Bag of Tricks

Instructional Activities & Games

Janet Blake
Jordan School District, Utah

Susan Ryberg
University of Utah

Joan Sebastian
University of Utah

LOVE PUBLISHING COMPANY
Denver, Colorado 80222

INSTRUCTIONAL TEACHING AIDS SERIES

Copyright © 1976 Love Publishing Company
Printed in the U. S. A.
ISBN 0-89108-062-7
Library of Congress Catalog Card Number 75-33558
10 9 8 7 6 5 4 3 2

CONTENTS

ACKNOWLEDGMENTS

It would be a virtual impossibility to mention all of the sources and individuals that have contributed ideas over the years which ultimately found their way, in some form, to the pages of this book. As with any project, however, there are certain individuals who have contributed in such a way that a particular expression of appreciation is in order. A very special thanks to Joyce Stavros Winn who was a major motivating force and who was instrumental in starting a partnership that has been highly productive as well as satisfying. The authors also wish to express sincere appreciation to Bette Farrell, Carol Neilsen, and Carol Gill. There is always one influential person who contributes in a way that stands out as crucial. This is certainly the case with the present volume and that special person is Dr. Cyrus W. Freston. It was he that provided the opportunity and encouragement for the authors to begin compiling the material presented herein. We are very grateful for his vision and assistance in so many ways. We would also like to extend special recognition to Dr. Clifford J. Drew for his expertise in editing the manuscript. We are indebted to him for his invaluable suggestions. Without the assistance of these individuals it is doubtful that the collection of activities found herein would have been put on paper and compiled for the use of others.

JS
SR
JB

INTRODUCTION

The present volume is divided into three broad sections: language activities, mathematics activities and game boards. The language section involves a variety of target areas including reading, writing and spelling skills. The mathematics section includes work on basic arithmetic operations such as addition, subtraction, multiplication and division. These operations are placed in a variety of contexts which are designed to facilitate instruction as well as build interest in the student by avoiding the deadly-dull format often encountered in math instruction. The third section, game boards, presents activities that are relevant to a variety of skill areas. This section may be viewed as an augmentation of the two previous sections in that skills initially acquired can be further reinforced in another context. Game boards may also be used to instruct in new skill areas where the format is particularly appropriate.

IMAGINATION AND CREATIVITY

This volume represents a compilation of activities and instructional strategies that have been devised, adapted and field tested over some nine collective years of experience by the authors. They have proven successful in a variety of settings with a broad range of students. In some cases the students were encountering problems in a particular academic area while in others, the activities represented an exciting variation for students who were essentially progressing satisfactorily in their academic programs. In all cases the activities represented a delightful addition to the teacher's bag of tricks which provided a productive change for student and teacher alike. Many of the activities have also proven very useful in work with parents who were either concerned about a particular skill area or just wanted to work with their child on something to help in building that crucial parent-child relationship.

One very important purpose of this book has already been addressed, that of suggesting a variety of instructional materials and activities. There is a second purpose, however, which holds equal if not greater importance in the view of the authors. This purpose is the triggering of the imagination and creativity of the user, whether it be teacher, parent or friend. Developing and adapting the various activities in ways that are most suitable for the particular situation involved is encouraged. This may mean the particular child, materials available, educational setting or adaptations that simply are satisfying to the user's creative urges. Obviously no single book can be produced that meets the needs of all possible situations. Consequently, if the requirements of all or even most situations are to be met, the reader must modify, adapt, and even create. Encouraging creative adaptation has another motive, however, which goes beyond merely meeting situational needs. The process of becoming more creative requires an individual to become increasingly skilled at analyzing a given task. This skill, in turn, enhances many dimensions of the teacher's ability to instruct effectively. Throughout the text the authors have repeatedly attempted to prompt adaptation by the user. This accounts for the recurrence of the use of "etc." and other similar phrases. Experience suggests that flexibility and adaptability are very important elements in any set of suggestions. One unique aspect of this volume is the adaptability of the activities in terms of child skill level, user resources and the setting in which they may be used.

Each activity that is discussed in this volume represents an item that is inexpensive and easily constructed. Such considerations are often very important in situations where limited budgets are available and/or the availability of material resources is restricted. This area of concern may well be foremost in geographically rural and remote areas as well as urban environments where a vast resource base is not available. The authors' intent is that the user's creativity be the crucial resource in determining how rich or how restricted the instructional environment is for the children being served. This is issued as a challenge to the reader; there really is no compelling reason why your protégé cannot have as rich an educational environment as any other child. It should also be noted that creation of activities and materials can be a highly satisfying and a rewarding endeavor for readers who do not find themselves in situations where budgets or resources are limited (wherever that might be).

CHECKLISTS OF APTITUDES AND SKILLS

The reader will note two checklists presented in matrix form which are found at the front of Sections One and Two. Terminology used throughout these checklists has been drawn from both special education as well as regular education. For example, such nomenclature as auditory and visual motor channels essentially comes from the special education arena. These same approaches, however, have proven very useful with children who do not have learning problems. Likewise, many ideas that were developed in regular education have been helpful in the task of teaching the child with learning difficulties. It is the basic philosophy of the authors that effective instructional techniques must be identified and utilized regardless of origin. Because of this posture, no single model has been adopted in the compilation of this book. Instead, an operational format has been adopted which represents a composite of several models and approaches. Since a composite format is used the reader is strongly encouraged to review the definition section (see the Appendix). In some cases definitions may involve seemingly subtle but important points which will make the use of this volume more effective.

The checklists are provided as a reference for the user so that an activity can be quickly and easily identified according to a given child's particular skill level and learning style. These checklists should not, however, be considered as ironclad guides that might become restrictive. If this occurs, the adaptive value of the volume will be lost and an important purpose of the book diminished. Use the checklists as general guides with the constant knowledge that activities may be modified effectively to serve other objectives.

It also should be noted that the materials suggested for activities throughout the text may be interchanged depending upon their availability. The suggestions found herein represent materials that have been successfully used in the past. Frequently construction paper may be used in place of oaktag, or oaktag may be used in lieu of poster board, etc. Additionally, the reader will often find references such as laminating equipment or clear contact paper. Laminating equipment, while available in many school districts, is frequently somewhat inaccessible. Therefore, clear contact paper is suggested and can be purchased in most department or variety stores.

SECTION ONE
LANGUAGE

LANGUAGE CHECKLIST

LEARNING APTITUDES

ACTIVITY/GAME		Auditory				Visual						Response Required	
		Auditory Reception*	Auditory Association*	Auditory Memory*	Auditory Discrimination*	Visual Reception*	Visual Association*	Visual Memory*	Visual Closure*	Visual Discrimination*	Visual Sequencing*	Verbal Response*	Manual Response*
Words 'N Tunes	p. 15	✓	✓	✓+	✓+			✓	✓				✓
Bones	p. 16					✓	✓	✓	✓+	✓+		✓	✓
String Match	p. 18					✓	✓+			✓+			✓
Matching Letters	p. 20					✓	✓+			✓+			✓
Door	p. 21	✓	✓	✓		✓+		✓	✓	✓+			✓
Alphabet Worm	p. 22			✓+		✓		✓		✓	✓+		✓
Who What Where	p. 24		✓+			✓	✓			✓	✓+	✓	✓
Sentence Roll	p. 25		✓+			✓				✓	✓+		✓
Word Search	p. 26	✓	✓	✓+		✓	✓	✓		✓+		✓	✓
Confusion	p. 28	✓				✓	✓			✓+		✓	✓
Monster Words	p. 30					✓					✓+		✓
Shifty Short Vowels	p. 32				✓	✓	✓			✓+		✓	✓
Dot to Dot	p. 34					✓			✓+	✓+	✓		✓
Blindfold Games	p. 36	✓	✓	✓+				✓+				✓	✓
Bingo Games	p. 38	✓	✓	✓+	✓	✓	✓			✓+			✓
Dig and Spell	p. 40	✓		✓		✓	✓	✓+		✓+	✓+		✓
Wooden Language Cubes	p. 41	✓	✓	✓	✓	✓	✓			✓+	✓+	✓	✓
Tangle	p. 42	✓		✓+	✓	✓	✓			✓+			✓
Letter Shuffle	p. 44					✓	✓	✓		✓+	✓+		✓
Cartoon Strips	p. 46					✓+	✓				✓+		✓
Card Slap	p. 47	✓	✓	✓	✓	✓	✓	✓		✓+			✓
Creative Writing Wheels	p. 48					✓+	✓						✓
Ladder Game	p. 50					✓				✓		✓	
Memory	p. 51							✓+				✓	
Word Block	p. 52					✓		✓				✓	✓
Go Fish	p. 54	✓				✓	✓			✓+		✓	
Alphabet Train	p. 55					✓	✓		✓+		✓		✓

✓+ Primary Emphasis of Activity
✓ Involved but not Primary
* Defined in Appendix

	READING SKILLS							LANGUAGE SKILLS					MOTOR SKILLS				
Sound blending	Consonants	Vowels	Sound-Symbol Relationship	Dictionary Skills	Comprehension Skills	Sight Words*		Spelling	Handwriting	Creative Writing	Parts of Speech	Sentences	Gross Motor*	Fine Motor*	Visual Motor*	Appropriate for Secondary	Easily Adapted for Secondary
	✓	✓						✓	✓		✓+			✓	✓	✓	✓
	✓+	✓+	✓+			✓+									✓+		
				✓	✓	✓								✓+	✓+		
														✓	✓		
													✓	✓+	✓		
														✓	✓		
									✓		✓+	✓+		✓	✓		
									✓		✓+	✓+		✓	✓		
✓	✓+	✓+	✓+					✓	✓					✓	✓	✓	✓
	✓	✓				✓											
✓+	✓	✓	✓+											✓			
	✓	✓+															
	✓													✓	✓+		
✓	✓+	✓+				✓								✓+			
	✓	✓	✓+			✓								✓	✓		
	✓	✓						✓+						✓			✓
✓+	✓+	✓+	✓+					✓	✓					✓	✓		
	✓+	✓+	✓+			✓							✓+				
	✓	✓						✓+	✓				✓	✓	✓	✓	✓
				✓				✓	✓	✓+		✓+		✓	✓	✓	✓
	✓+	✓+	✓+			✓+							✓				
				✓				✓	✓	✓+		✓+		✓	✓	✓	✓
	✓+	✓+	✓+			✓+											
	✓+	✓+				✓+											
	✓+	✓+	✓+			✓+								✓	✓		
	✓+	✓+				✓+											
														✓	✓		

WORDS 'N TUNES

SKILLS Consonants, Vowels, Spelling, Handwriting, Parts of Speech, Fine Motor, Visual Motor.

MATERIALS Popular records appropriate to age level, record player.

SUGGESTED ACTIVITIES

1. The example illustrates a way to work on parts of speech using "Jingle Bells." Type out the first letter for each noun in the song and accompany it with a blank for the child to complete. As the child listens to the song, he identifies each noun using the first letter as a clue. He then completes the blank with the rest of the word. For example, the first blank would be *snow,* then *horse,* etc. The song may need to be played two or three times.

2. Play as described in number one above but listening for verbs, vowel sounds, etc.

3. Provide the children with a key word that is not in the song you have chosen and have them write all the words they hear that rhyme with the key word.

4. The children could simply tally how many times they hear a particular sound or word in a song. This would eliminate the writing aspect which may be difficult for some children.

Jingle Bells

S _____	B _____	H _____	B _____	H _____	W _____
H _____	B _____	S _____	B _____	S _____	F _____
S _____	S _____		W _____	B _____	H _____
F _____	F _____		F _____	B _____	S _____

BONES

SKILLS Consonants, Vowels, Sound-Symbol Relationship, Sight Words, Visual-Motor.

MATERIALS Oaktag, magic marker, dice, envelopes.

DIRECTIONS Reproduce the skeleton to the appropriate size needed on oaktag. Number the pieces according to the diagram. Laminate or cover them with clear contact paper. Cut out and put pieces into an envelope.

SUGGESTED ACTIVITIES

1. Each child should have an envelope with the skeleton pieces and a die numbered from 1 to 6. Write words, letters, number combinations, etc., on the individual pieces. The child throws the die and finds the appropriate skeleton piece. He must say the word, letter, number combination, etc. If he is correct, he keeps the piece in front of him. The first child to build his skeleton wins. The child may or may not use the picture of the skeleton to aid him in reproducing the figure.

2. To vary the activity, use animals, paper dolls, objects, etc., in place of a skeleton.

BONES

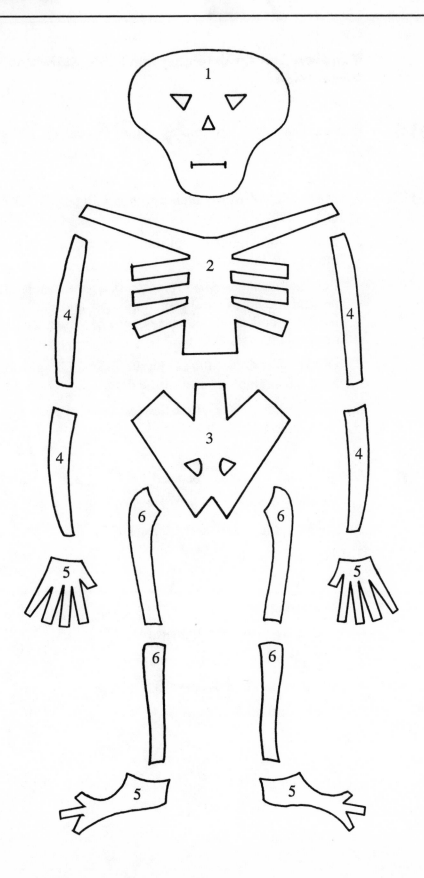

STRING MATCH

SKILLS Dictionary Skills, Comprehension Skills, Sight Words, Fine Motor, Visual Motor.

MATERIALS Rectangular cardboard pieces about 14 by 18 inches, shoelaces or yarn, gummed reinforcers.

DIRECTIONS
1. Make a list of words such as the months of the year on the left side of a card.
2. Make a knot at one end of the shoelace or yarn and punch a hole at the end of the word.
3. Put one of the gummed reinforcers over the hole (these reinforcers prevent the hole from becoming larger and make it easier to thread the other end of the shoelace or yarn), and then draw the shoelace or yarn through the hole.
4. On the right side of the card write the matching word in mixed order as in the example shown in the diagram.
5. Punch a hole to the left of these words and put gummed reinforcer on the hole.

SUGGESTED ACTIVITIES The following ideas may be used for string match activities:
1. Months of the year and abbreviations
2. Days of the week and abbreviations
3. Rhyming words
4. Opposites
5. Compound words
6. Arabic and Roman numerals
7. Multiplication facts and answers
8. Addition facts and answers
9. Words and their meanings

STRING MATCH

MONTHS OF THE YEAR

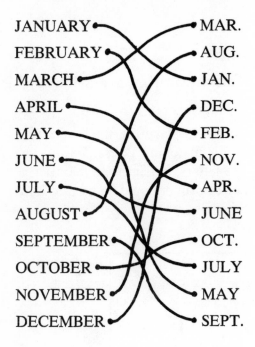

JANUARY	MAR.
FEBRUARY	AUG.
MARCH	JAN.
APRIL	DEC.
MAY	FEB.
JUNE	NOV.
JULY	APR.
AUGUST	JUNE
SEPTEMBER	OCT.
OCTOBER	JULY
NOVEMBER	MAY
DECEMBER	SEPT.

DAYS OF THE WEEK

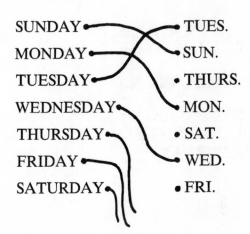

SUNDAY	TUES.
MONDAY	SUN.
TUESDAY	THURS.
WEDNESDAY	MON.
THURSDAY	SAT.
FRIDAY	WED.
SATURDAY	FRI.

RHYMES

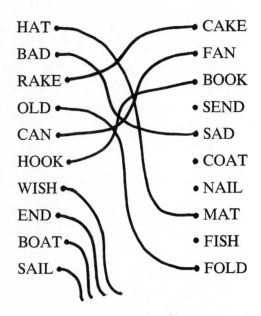

HAT	CAKE
BAD	FAN
RAKE	BOOK
OLD	SEND
CAN	SAD
HOOK	COAT
WISH	NAIL
END	MAT
BOAT	FISH
SAIL	FOLD

OPPOSITES

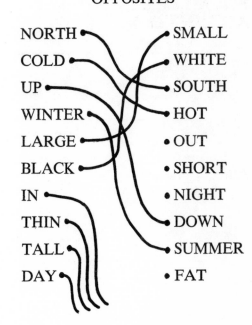

NORTH	SMALL
COLD	WHITE
UP	SOUTH
WINTER	HOT
LARGE	OUT
BLACK	SHORT
IN	NIGHT
THIN	DOWN
TALL	SUMMER
DAY	FAT

MATCHING LETTERS

SKILLS   Fine Motor, Visual Motor.

MATERIALS   Oaktag, magic marker.

DIRECTIONS   Cut twenty-six oaktag cards 3″ by 6″ and twenty-six that are 2″ by 2½″.

SUGGESTED ACTIVITY   This is a matching activity. The object is to place the smaller card on top of the larger card to come up with matching pairs. Lower case letters can be matched with upper case letters, cursive with manuscript, etc. See the diagram. A stop watch or egg timer could be used to build speed.

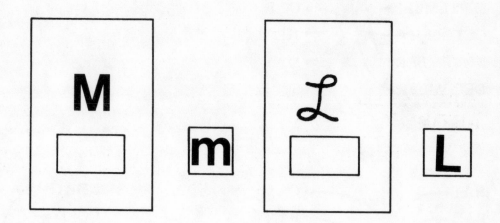

DOOR

SKILLS Gross Motor, Fine Motor, Visual Motor.

MATERIALS Oaktag, magic marker, masking tape (optional depending on the manner of presentation).

DIRECTIONS

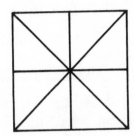

The above design can be made on the chalk board, on the floor with masking tape, or on a piece of oaktag which is then laminated.

SUGGESTED ACTIVITY The object is to find the letters of the alphabet (e.g., Z, N, E) that are embedded in the figure on the door design. Children can perform in a number of ways such as tracing the letter design with their finger as the teacher calls out the letter to be found. If the door is designed on the floor with masking tape, the children may walk the lines that are relevant for the hidden letter. This can be done as an individual activity or with a group as the teacher calls out the letter to be found. Teams may be formed with points awarded for correct responses.

ALPHABET WORM

SKILLS   Fine Motor, Visual Motor.

MATERIALS   Oaktag, magic markers, construction paper, grease pencil.

DIRECTIONS   Put the picture on a 9″ x 12″ sheet of oaktag. Put words or letters on round circles of construction paper that are the same size as the circles on the worm. Put these circles into an envelope.

SUGGESTED ACTIVITIES

1. The child places circles in alphabetical order on the worm.

2. Laminate the oaktag and have the child write the words in alphabetical order with a grease pencil.

3. In order to use this game with a group of older children give each child an alphabet worm picture (similar to the diagram). Begin by having each player draw (without looking) five word circles at random. Each player should then place the five word circles face up on the worm in the order that they were drawn, putting one circle in each space. The remaining circles should then be stacked face down to be used as a drawing pile. The object of this game is to put the word circles in alphabetical order by substituting words on the worm with words from the drawing pile. Note: words on the board cannot be replaced with each other. Players take turns drawing one card from the drawing pile. They may choose to replace that word with a word circle on their board if it will help in sequencing the words. If the player does not want the word, it is then discarded in a pile. A player's board may look like Figure 1 after

22

ALPHABET WORM

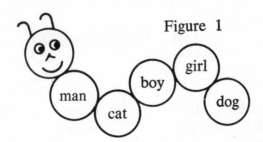

Figure 1

the initial placement of the five word circles. If a player on his turn draws the word *apple* he would want to replace the *man* circle word with *apple* since a comes before c in cat. See Turn 1. On his next

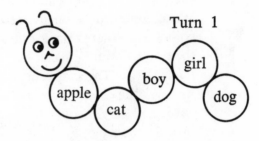

Turn 1

turn he might draw *farm*. His best play would be to now remove *boy* and replace it with *farm*. See Turn 2 in the diagram. At this point the words are alphabetically ordered with the exception of the

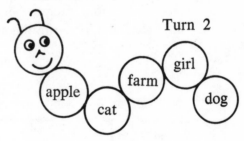

Turn 2

dog circle. This player will continue until he draws a word which he can replace with dog, in other words, a word that begins with an h, i, j, k, etc.

WHO, WHAT, WHERE

SKILLS   Parts of Speech, Handwriting, Sentences, Fine Motor, Visual Motor.

MATERIALS   Three envelopes, three different colors of construction paper, felt tip pen.

DIRECTIONS   Write Who, What, and Where, separately on three envelopes. Cut the construction paper into squares or rectangles that are the right size to fit in the envelopes. Take sentences from children's readers and divide each sentence into its subject (who), verb (what), and object (where). Write these words on the colored cards, placing all the Whos on one color, the Wheres on a different color, etc. Then put the cards into their appropriate envelopes. For example, suppose the sentence in the reader says "The cat went home." *The cat* would be written on a card that was the color you had chosen for Whos. *Went* would be on a What card, and *home* would be on a Where card. All would be in their appropriate envelopes.

SUGGESTED ACTIVITY   This is an activity to get children involved in writing and discovering sentence formation. The child draws one strip from each of the three envelopes and arranges them into a sentence in front of him. He then may read and/or write the sentence.

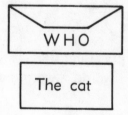
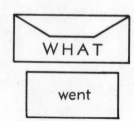

SENTENCE ROLL

SKILLS   Parts of Speech, Handwriting, Sentences, Fine Motor, Visual Motor.

MATERIALS   Four ¾" hard wood cubes—sanded.

DIRECTIONS   With a felt tip pen, write the following words on each cube:

      Cube 1: the, the, the, a, a, a
      Cube 2: bat, man, dog, rat, cat, dad
      Cube 3: was, got, went, is, is, was
      Cube 4: red, big, hot, mad, fat, little

When making this game it is best to keep in mind that an article cube, a noun cube, a verb cube, and an object cube are needed. When increasing the length of the sentences, several adjective cubes may be added.

SUGGESTED ACTIVITY   The child shakes the four cubes and arranges them into a sentence. After four word sequences are mastered, you may add more cubes with new words to increase the length of the sentence. The child may be timed, or required to write the sentence after he has arranged the cubes.

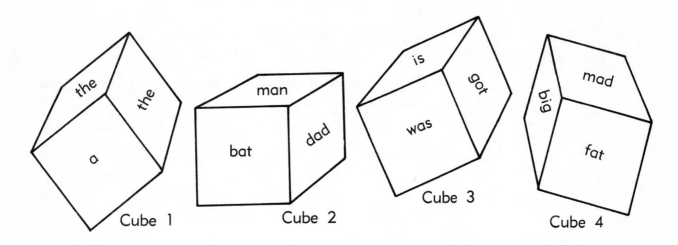

Cube 1   Cube 2   Cube 3   Cube 4

WORD SEARCH

SKILLS   Sound Blending, Consonants, Vowels, Sound-Symbol Relationship, Spelling, Handwriting, Fine Motor, Visual Motor.

MATERIALS   Ditto masters, graph paper, primer typewriter.

DIRECTIONS   On a piece of graph paper block off a square fifteen by fifteen blocks. Decide what phonetic skill is to be reinforced. For example, one word search could be *bl* words. Think of approximately twenty *bl* words. Write these words on the graph paper, one letter to a square. See the example in the diagram. Words may go across or down and may overlap. Fill in the remaining blank squares with letters of the alphabet, any order. Now transfer this to the ditto master. Do not transfer the lines; the graph paper was used only to assist in designing. To transfer, type (primer typewriter if possible) the letters in their appropriate position across and down the page. Two spaces between each letter (going across) and double spacing between lines is about right for the primer typewriter on regular sized paper.

SUGGESTED ACTIVITIES

1. The child circles all the bl combinations.

2. The child circles all the bl words he can find.

3. The child is given the bl words orally or in written form and then finds them.

4. The child puts all the bl words in alphabetical order after circling them.

5. This activity can be used with all phonetic skills, e.g., vowels, diagraphs, endings.

WORD SEARCH

```
B  B  L  A  C  K  P  L  G  B  L  A  D  E  S
F  L  T  X  V  B  L  G  N  K  E  T  Y  X  H
K  O  R  S  T  U  W  Z  N  B  B  L  O  C  K
A  W  M  B  L  A  D  E  X  B  V  U  T  S  M
J  P  O  K  H  F  C  Q  B  L  A  S  T  R  B
I  M  N  G  E  D  B  Z  Y  A  I  O  P  L  L
B  L  O  S  S  O  M  Y  Z  C  E  K  N  H  O
P  S  X  V  O  B  L  A  N  K  G  M  J  F  N
N  U  W  T  A  L  L  T  X  B  N  B  B  D  D
B  L  U  E  R  I  D  E  F  C  B  L  U  F  F
W  M  L  K  H  S  S  W  A  G  Y  A  I  D  C
S  C  B  J  D  T  S  Z  A  H  U  N  I  F  U
O  E  I  G  I  E  M  V  R  O  K  K  G  H  X
E  A  E  B  F  R  J  B  L  A  X  E  B  E  I
A  J  D  R  B  L  E  A  C  H  V  Z  A  N  G
```

ACROSS	DOWN
_____	_____
_____	_____
_____	_____
_____	_____
_____	_____
_____	_____
_____	_____
_____	_____
_____	_____

CONFUSION

SKILLS Consonants, Vowels, Sight Words.

MATERIALS Oaktag, magic marker.

DIRECTIONS Cut the oaktag into rectangular cards, 2½″ by 4″. Divide the cards into decks or packs with thirty-two cards in each. As many packs may be made as desired. For each pack, select from their readers those words that children easily confuse. See the diagram. Note the sample words for the packs below.

Begin by taking four blank cards and write the appropriate words on them as in the diagram below. Note that these words are from series one of the sample pack words on page 28. There are eight series in each pack which makes a total of 32 cards. Continue the process until each series in pack one is completed. Complete the other packs in the same way.

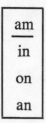
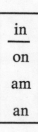

on	an	am	in
an	am	in	on
am	in	on	am
in	on	an	an

Sample Words for the Packs

Pack 1

1. on, an, am, in
2. his, her, he, his
3. on, now, no, one
4. was, see, saw, we
5. my, may, man, many
6. came, come, coming, comes
7. when, what, which, where
8. who, how, new, here

Pack 2

1. four, of, for, from
2. three, their, they, there
3. you, young, year, your
4. than, then, the, them
5. have, has, had, having
6. using, us, used, use
7. hand, hard, head, heard
8. third, thank, think, thing

CONFUSION

Pack 3

1. hold, held, help, helps
2. would, world, work, word
3. while, write, white, whole
4. want, went, were, wear
5. fall, fell, fill, full
6. close, class, clean, clear
7. house, horse, horn, home
8. ball, bell, hill, bill

Pack 4

1. does, done, don't, didn't
2. lost, last, least, left
3. stone, store, story, study
4. bread, break, broken, brother
5. through, throw, thought, though
6. shut, shot, shoot, short
7. hadn't, hasn't, wasn't, haven't
8. were, warm, war, wear

SUGGESTED ACTIVITY

Three to five students play together using one pack. Five cards are dealt to each player. The first player looks at the cards in his hand. Suppose he had the first two cards in the illustration dealt to him. He would then figure out the other cards needed in the series to complete the set, and ask for them in his turn. For instance, he would know that either the *am* or the *in* card was needed. He would ask another player, "Do you have the *am* card?" If the other player does not have the *am* card then the player would draw one card from the remaining face down cards in the center of the table. When a player has collected all four of the cards in a series, he lays them down and says each word in the series. The first player to get rid of his cards is the winner.

MONSTER WORDS

SKILLS   Sound Blending, Consonants, Vowels, Sound-Symbol Relationship, Fine Motor.

MATERIALS   Construction paper, magic marker, ¾″ sanded wooden cube to be used as a die.

DIRECTIONS   Divide animal bodies (or monster bodies, or make up your own) into three sections—a head, a torso and a tail. Trace or draw the different parts onto construction paper and cut out. On the heads write a beginning consonant, a beginning digraph or a beginning blend. On the torso write a vowel, or a vowel team. On the tail write an ending consonant, an ending digraph or an ending blend. See the diagram. On the sides of a die write the words head, torso and tail.

SUGGESTED ACTIVITY   Two or more should play this game. Put body parts into piles with all the heads together, all the torsos together, etc. The first player rolls the die and draws the top card from the appropriate pile as indicated by the die. The die is then given to the next player. When a player obtains all three body parts he puts them together and blends the word. He then puts his animal to the side. The player who makes the most words in a set time period wins. Depending on the skill level of the players nonsense and/or real words may be used.

MONSTER WORDS

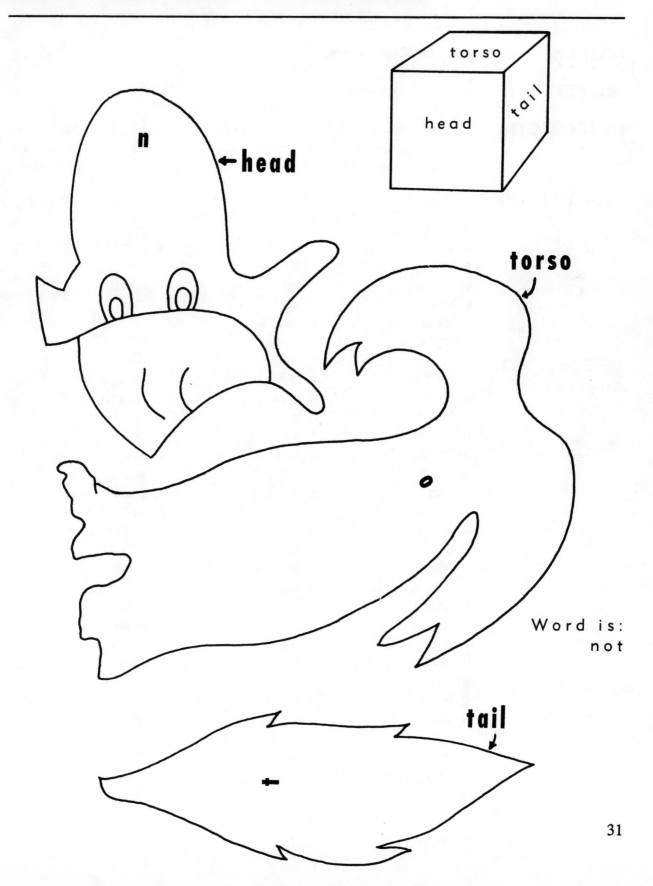

torso

head

tail

n

←head

torso

Word is:
not

tail

t

SHIFTY SHORT VOWELS

SKILLS   **Vowels, Consonants.**

MATERIALS   Oaktag, magic marker.

DIRECTIONS   Cut the oaktag into 2½″ by 4″ cards. A total of 123 cards will be needed. These cards will constitute three different decks, one each for the lists of words below.

Deck 1	*Deck 2*	*Deck 3*
e pet e	e peck e	e pep e
e set e	e pen e	e better e
e bed e	e deck e	e peddle e
e met e	e ten e	e blend e
e hem e	e leg e	e mess e
e fen e	a lack a	e left e
e beg e	a mast a	e net e
e net e	a stack a	a rat a
a ham a	a tan a	a mass a
a sat a	a pack a	a rack a
a bag a	a pan a	a strap a
a bat a	a jab a	a bland a
a fan a	a tack a	a sang a
a pat a	a lag a	a sap a
a sack a	a clack a	a paddle a
a mat a	u jug u	a packer a
a hat a	u stuck u	a batter a
a bad a	u must u	u sup u
u bug u	u luck u	u muss u
u mutt u	u cluck u	u pup u
u suck u	u duck u	u butter u
u but u	u pun u	u sung u
u fun u	u lug u	u rut u
u hum u	u tuck u	n nut u
u bud u	u tub u	u puddle u
u hut u	i pin i	u pluck u
n nut u	i mist i	u pucker u
i bid i	i pick i	i sing i
i mitt i	i click i	i bid i
i sit i	i stick i	i miss i
i sick i	i jig i	i fiddle i

SHIFTY SHORT VOWELS

Deck 1	Deck 2	Deck 3
i hit i	i lick i	i strip i
i him i	i tick i	i pip i
i fin i	o dot o	i rick i
i pit i	o lock o	i bitter i
i bit i	o stock o	i nit i
o sock o	o clock o	i picker i
o pot o	o jog o	i sip i
o hot o	o fog o	o rock o
o not o	o log o	o pop o
o bog o	o pock o	o rot o

Using the magic marker, write words on both ends of each card in the fashion shown in the diagram. Make a card such as this for each word in the first deck. Continue in the same manner until all three decks are constructed.

Example of card

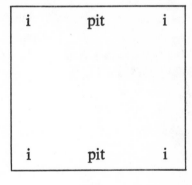

SUGGESTED ACTIVITY

Three or four players are needed. Using one deck, deal five cards to each player and put the rest of the cards face down in a pile in the center of the table. Turn the top card face up. Play the game as you do Crazy Eights. The first player looks at the card that is face up and tries to match it with a card in his hand. He may match the card in one of two ways, by matching the card with one in his hand that has the same vowel (e.g., pet with set), or by matching cards that have all the letters the same *except* the vowel (e.g., pet with pit). When he makes a match he must say the words. He then lays his card down. If no card in the player's hand matches the face-up card, he must draw from the center pile until he draws one that does match. The first player to get rid of all his cards is the winner.

DOT TO DOT

SKILLS Vowels, Fine Motor, Visual Motor.

MATERIALS Dot to dot pictures, tracing paper, ditto masters.

DIRECTIONS Begin with a simple dot to dot picture—one with approximately twenty dots. Trace the dots from the dot to dot picture on the ditto master, omitting the numbers. If the dot to dot picture selected has twenty-three dots, number a piece of scratch paper to forty. An additional seventeen distracting dots will later be placed on the ditto. Select twenty-three long vowel words and randomly place them on the list of forty. Number the dot to dot picture according to the numbers designated by the long vowel words on the master list. For example the dots may be numbered 1, 3, 6, 9, etc. See the example diagram. Now add the distracting dots on the ditto and number them accordingly to complete the sequence (e.g., 2, 4, 5, 7, 8, etc.). On the master list these would be words other than long vowel words. The numbers are used because they correspond with the example. Fewer distracting dots may be chosen.

SUGGESTED ACTIVITIES

1. The child reads the master list of words and connects dots which correspond with long vowel words in order to complete the picture. For example, the child would connect dot number 1 to dot number 3 omitting dot number 2 because it isn't a long vowel word.

2. This could be adapted using short vowel words, vowel teams, multiples of a certain number, numbers that can be divided by a certain number, etc.

Use only numbers from the words with long vowels to do dot to dot picture on the following page.

1. meek	11. whale	21. pope	31. rush
2. sat	12. snip	22. hope	32. sneak
3. steam	13. tame	23. tap	33. eagle
4. pin	14. hug	24. dude	34. track
5. pet	15. snipe	25. these	35. drip
6. meat	16. huge	26. rot	36. beaver
7. wag	17. fin	27. joke	37. grab
8. cut	18. price	28. not	38. note
9. treat	19. craze	29. lack	39. twice
10. plume	20. tube	30. probe	40. race

DOT TO DOT

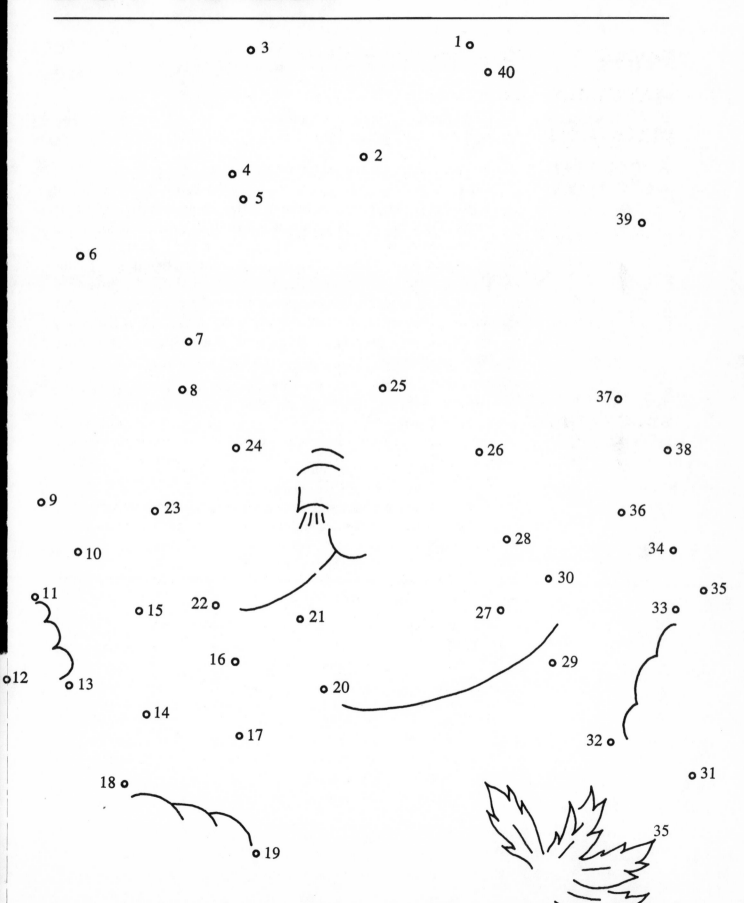

BLINDFOLD GAMES

SKILLS   Consonants, Vowels, Sound Blending, Sight Words, Fine Motor.

MATERIALS   Blindfold, tactile letters and/or numbers.

SUGGESTED ACTIVITIES

1. Partners take turns being blindfolded. The teacher or partner selects letters or numbers and places them on the floor. The other child then tries to figure out the sound, letter or number by feeling its form. The child should then respond orally. If he is correct, then he scores one point. Words and/or multi-digit numbers may also be placed on the floor. This is good memory practice since the child must retain each sound or number mentally as he progresses through the sequence. Game points may be given according to the number of letters or digits in the sequence. If desired, a timer may be used to limit the length of time a child may spend decoding the word or number.

2. Blindfolds are also good for work on identification of body parts and directionality. Blindfold one child and give commands similar to the following:

   a. "Touch my shoulders, head, foot, etc."
   b. "Touch your eyes, elbow, knee, etc."
   c. "Touch your left eye, ear, hand, etc."
   d. "Touch my left hand, leg, arm, etc."
   e. "Touch your left leg and my right arm."
   f. "Walk three steps forward and two steps to the left."
   g. "Walk two steps backwards and one step to the right."

BLINDFOLD GAMES

m a n   4   3   6

BINGO GAMES

SKILLS Sound-Symbol Relationship, Consonants, Vowels, Sight Words, Fine Motor, Visual Motor.

MATERIALS Poster board, magic marker, chips or small squares of paper for covering boxes, oaktag.

DIRECTIONS Make any size bingo card. It is best to leave the boxes blank and then laminate the card or cover it with clear contact paper. Cut the oaktag into rectangles 2½″ by 4″. Use these cards for the stimulus words or phrases.

SUGGESTED ACTIVITIES 1. *Regular Bingo.* Fill in the empty boxes with words, sounds, numbers, etc. that the child is currently studying. The same stimulus

BINGO

game	box	came	father	come
girl	was	ran	word	went
that	there	where	when	what
said	the	it	rat	blow
man	b	fat	boy	d

BINGO GAMES

words should also be written on the oaktag cards. The teacher or leader draws a card and calls out the word, sound, number, problem, etc. The child or children cover the appropriate box with a chip. For example:

    a. "Cover the word that rhymes with man."
    b. "Cover the word that has the same beginning sound (or vowel sound) as black."
    c. "Cover the answer to this problem: 4 x 5."
    d. "Cover this number: Six." Hold up the word card.

The first child to have five in a row calls out bingo. His answers should then be checked with the stimulus cards.

2. *Battleship Bingo.* Two or more children can play together. Put a partition of some sort between players so that the playing cards are concealed. The teacher fills in the boxes of two or more cards with the sounds, words, etc. being studied. Those same words should be written on individual cards for the drawing pile. Each player secretly places battleships (or chips) on a designated number of boxes. Players take turns drawing cards and reading the word or sound out loud. If a player reads a word that his partner or another player has covered with a battleship, then the battleship is knocked off the board. Players are eliminated from the game when they lose all of their battleships. The winner must have at least one remaining battleship.

Battleship Bingo

● man	pan	fan
Dan	ran	● Nan
fat	● nap	Sam

Battleship Bingo

fan	Nan	● Sam
● Pan	ran	nap
fat	Dan	● man

man	Drawing cards

DIG AND SPELL

SKILLS   Consonants, Vowels, Spelling, Fine Motor.

MATERIALS   Oaktag, alphabet chips or oaktag on which letters can be written.

DIRECTIONS   Cut the oaktag into 2½″ by 4″ cards. On the cards write directions such as: A three letter word that ends with 'n', A three letter word that starts with 'f', Any four letter word, An animal to ride, etc.

SUGGESTED ACTIVITIES

1. For two or more players put the alphabet chips face up on the table. One person picks up a "dig and spell" card and reads the direction. Each player then digs into the alphabet pile to find letters to make the word. The first player to make the word gets a point. The player with the most points at the end of the game is the winner. A set number of points to each card depending on its difficulty could be assigned.

2. For an individual activity play as described in number one above but have the child draw his own direction cards and spell the words. You may want to see how many words he can spell in ten minutes.

Direction Card

A three letter word that ends with t.

WOODEN LANGUAGE CUBES

SKILLS Sound Blending, Consonants, Vowels, Sound-Symbol Relationship, Spelling, Handwriting, Fine Motor, Visual Motor.

MATERIALS Felt tip markers, ¾″ hard wood cubes—sanded.

SUGGESTED ACTIVITIES

1. *Sound Cubes.* Put the sounds that are to be studied on the sides of the cube. Shake the cube or cubes on a table top for oral drill on sound recognition. This may be used in groups, individually or with partners. You may also want to combine sounds on cubes that will form words for a "spill and spell" type game. The child would then write the word after he spells it with the cubes. A stopwatch or timer may be used to increase rate.

2. *Letter Cubes.* This is the same as sound cubes but the children call out the names of the letters. Alternate capitals and lower case or cursive and manuscript letters on the sides of the cubes.

3. *Cube Grab.* Write letters, words, prefixes, suffices, etc. to be studied on the sides of the cubes. Shake the cubes on table top and call out a word, letter, etc. The children grab the correct cube. This may also be played with sound and letter cubes.

4. *Cube Blend.* This is the same as cube grab but blend the word out loud for the children to grab. For example, say "find mm—aa—t."

TANGLE

SKILLS Consonants, Vowels, Sound-Symbol Relationship, Sight Words, Gross Motor.

MATERIALS Oil cloth, magic marker, grease pencil, twenty cards 3″ by 5″.

DIRECTIONS Cut a large piece of oil cloth at least 3′ by 6′ similar to the popular commercial Twister game mat. With a magic marker, draw a grid on the oil cloth as shown in the diagram. The boxes should be large enough to hold a child's hand or foot. Using a grease pencil, write words, letters or whatever skill is being studied in the boxes of the Tangle mat. Be sure to randomly write each word twice on the mat. Write directions similar to the following on the direction cards:

    a. Put your left hand on man and your right foot on pan.
    b. Put your right hand on rat and your left hand on sat.

SUGGESTED ACTIVITIES

1. One child draws and reads a direction card for two players. The players follow the commands. The winner is the child who can keep his body (excluding hands and feet) from touching the floor.

2. For other instructional activities put letters, numbers, geometric shapes, etc. in the boxes of the Tangle mat. Construct appropriate direction cards and proceed as described above.

42

TANGLE

TANGLE

man	bat	fat	man
nap	tan	ham	nap
can	ham	tan	sat
sat	fat	bat	can

LETTER SHUFFLE

SKILLS   Consonants, Vowels, Spelling, Handwriting, Gross Motor, Fine Motor, Visual Motor.

MATERIALS   Large sheet of heavy paper or oil cloth, puck or disc, felt tip markers.

DIRECTIONS   The playing board (see the diagram) should measure eight feet long and seven feet wide including the border. Divide the board into six inch squares. This is only a suggested size and the board may be larger or smaller depending upon your needs. Write letters and their point values in each square as illustrated.

SUGGESTED ACTIVITY   Taking turns, each player shoots the puck or disc and then writes on paper the letter he hits. When all players have had ten shots, each player must then use his letters to make as many words as he can. Points are scored by adding the values of the letters used in words spelled correctly. The player with the most points is the winner.

LETTER SHUFFLE

A_2	U_4	B_4	G_5	N_4	Q_7	Z_7	E_2	I_2	W_6	P_5	Z_7	R_5	J_6	O_2
C_3	P_5	K_6	O_2	J_6	S_3	D_4	L_4	A_2	N_4	E_2	A_2	D_4	G_5	M_4
N_4	E_2	W_6	H_5	P_5	W_6	D_4	C_3	B_4	K_6	C_3	J_6	V_7	A_2	U_4
O_2	J_6	X_8	T_3	E_2	Y_6	M_4	Z_7	E_2	B_4	X_8	T_3	P_5	W_6	B_4
I_2	Z_7	G_3	F_4	A_2	C_3	I_2	H_5	U_4	L_4	S_3	R_5	I_2	E_2	Q_7
T_3	K_6	Q_7	R_4	M_4	G_5	L_4	M_4	I_2	O_2	G_5	N_4	B_4	Y_6	O_2
H_5	O_2	Z_7	E_2	C_3	I_2	J_6	P_5	E_2	W_7	A_2	S_3	L_4	H_5	T_3
A_2	Y_6	L_4	X_8	J_6	A_2	V_7	T_3	N_4	O_2	D_4	Z_7	S_3	P_5	E_2
D_4	H_5	O_2	S_3	N_4	K_6	E_2	O_2	Q_7	I_2	V_7	U_4	C_3	K_4	T_3
L_4	T_3	M_4	C_3	O_2	B_4	H_5	R_5	Y_6	K_6	L_4	Z_7	R_5	O_2	L_4
R_5	E_2	V_7	A_2	N_4	T_3	A_2	V_7	E_2	O_2	H_5	U_4	S_3	F_4	M_4
F_4	X_8	H_5	I_2	J_6	W_7	F_4	K_6	T_3	V_7	S_3	F_2	G_5	Y_6	I_2
S_3	U_4	A_2	E_2	C_3	R_5	M_4	I_2	X_8	M_4	J_6	W_6	R_5	A_2	P_5

CARTOON STRIPS

SKILLS

Comprehension, Spelling, Handwriting, Creative Writing, Sentences, Fine Motor, Visual Motor.

MATERIALS

Cartoon strips taken from comic books, magazines, newspapers, etc., clear contact paper or laminating equipment, construction paper, grease pencil.

DIRECTIONS

Cut off the captions from the cartoon strips. Paste the cartoon strip on a piece of construction paper and draw in the speech bubbles leaving them blank. Laminate the strips or cover with clear contact paper. Dittos can be made directly from black cartoon strips by using a thermofax machine.

SUGGESTED ACTIVITIES

1. To stimulate creative writing have the child take a cartoon strip and write in his own captions with a grease pencil.

2. Cut the cartoon strip into its frames. Have the child take the frames and arrange them into the correct sequence. The captions may be left in the speech bubbles for this activity.

CARD SLAP

SKILLS   **Consonants, Vowels, Sound-Symbol Relationship, Sight Words, Gross Motor.**

MATERIALS   Oaktag flash cards (any size), magic markers.

DIRECTIONS   Write the words or sounds to be studied on the flash cards.

SUGGESTED ACTIVITIES

1. Spread the word cards out on the table or floor. Call out a word (or sound). The first child to slap the word card keeps it. The child with the most cards at the end of the game is the winner. To vary the activity, call out words that aren't there. If a child slaps the wrong word, he must return one of his to the floor or table.

2. The word may also be spelled aloud. For example, "Find b—a—t" or, "Slap a word that begins like boat" or, "Slap the sound at the beginning of this word—boat."

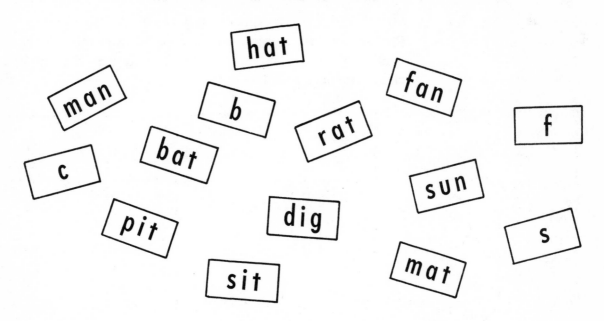

CREATIVE WRITING WHEELS

SKILLS   Comprehension, Spelling, Handwriting, Creative Writing, Sentences, Fine Motor, Visual Motor.

MATERIALS   Three spinners (see directions for spinners, page 99), small pictures from workbooks to be pasted in the sections of the spinners.

DIRECTIONS   Make three spinners approximately eight inches in diameter. Divide each spinner into eight pie shaped sections. In each section, glue a different picture. Do this for all three spinners.

SUGGESTED ACTIVITIES

1. Have the child spin each spinner. The three dials will be pointing to three different pictures. The child must then create a story around the three pictures. For example, the first spinner dial may be pointing to a dog, the second an airplane, and the third an elephant. His story must involve the dog, the airplane, and the elephant. The child may write his story or dictate it into a tape recorder.

2. Play as described in number one above but vary the number of spinners used. The number of spinners used may depend upon the child's age and skill level.

CREATIVE WRITING WHEELS

LADDER GAME

SKILLS   Consonants, Vowels, Sound-Symbol Relationship, Sight Words.

MATERIALS   Oaktag flash cards (any size), die numbered 1 through 6, position markers.

DIRECTIONS   Have each child line up his word cards on the table top or floor to resemble a ladder. See the diagram. Each child puts out the same number of cards.

SUGGESTED ACTIVITIES

1. The first player shakes the die and moves his marker up his ladder the designated number of places. If he says the word correctly, (a time limit can be put on him—5 seconds) then he removes the card from his ladder. The first child to get rid of his ladder is the winner. For variation line up the word cards face down.

2. Use sound cards instead of word cards.

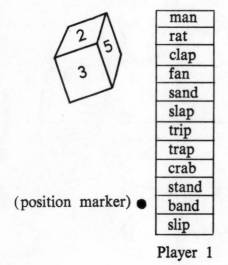

| man |
| rat |
| clap |
| fan |
| sand |
| slap |
| trip |
| trap |
| crab |
| stand |
| band |
| slip |

(position marker) ●

Player 1

| strap |
| stand |
| bark |
| card |
| dark |
| tray |
| last |
| blast |
| start |
| yard |
| mark |
| farm |

● (position marker)

Player 2

MEMORY

SKILLS   **Consonants, Vowels, Sight Words.**

MATERIALS   An even number of flash cards (e.g., 10, 12, etc.), magic marker.

DIRECTIONS   Write words or sounds on flash cards. Make two cards for each word or sound. Clip the right hand corner of the cards as in the diagram so cards may be easily sorted.

SUGGESTED ACTIVITIES

1. *Plain Memory.* Shuffle the cards and place them face down in rows on a table or on the floor as in the diagram. Each player, taking turns, draws two cards and reads each word out loud. If the words match, the child keeps the pair. If it is not a match, the cards are returned face down to their original position. The player with the most pairs at the end of the game is the winner. Note: The total number of words used should be determined on the basis of the child's level. Ordinarily, begin with a few pairs and gradually increase the number.

2. *Other Memory Games.*
   a. Play as described in number one above but use rhyming pairs (e.g., hat matches with mat, etc.).
   b. Play as described above but use vowel pairs, consonant pairs (e.g., h*a*t matches with m*a*n) or initial sounds (*sl*ap matches with *sl*op).
   c. For math practice make pairs of cards using the problem and the answer or the number and the word (e.g., 4 + 5 matches with 9; or 4 matches with FOUR).

WORD BLOCK

SKILLS
Consonants, Vowels, Sound-Symbol Relationship, Sight Words, Fine Motor, Visual Motor.

MATERIALS
Clear plastic sheet 56″ square or large sheet of poster paper, magic marker, flash cards (two sets in two different colors), clear contact paper or laminate.

DIRECTIONS
Mark the plastic off into 4″ by 4″ squares with a magic marker making a total of 196 squares. Make two sets of flash cards, each set a different color. The flash cards should measure 4″ by 4″ in order to fit into the squares on the plastic sheet. If the cards are laminated or covered with clear contact paper before writing on them, they can be reused with different words.

SUGGESTED ACTIVITIES

1. Two children can play this activity. Each child has his own set of flash cards. For example, one child would have blue cards with his words on them and the other child would have red cards with his own set of words. Taking turns, each child draws a word from his stack, reads it, and if correct can place it on the plastic grid. The object of the game is to be the first player to get five cards in a row either horizontally, vertically or diagonally, while at the same time, blocking his opponent from obtaining five in a row. If the child misreads his word, he puts it on the bottom of his stack and loses his turn.

2. Follow the same procedure as in number one but put math problems, sounds, etc. on the flash cards.

WORD BLOCK

WORD BLOCK

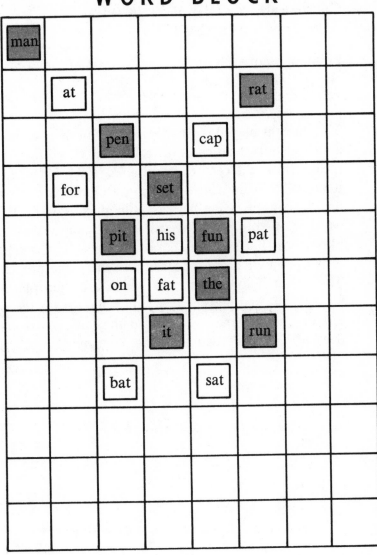

GO FISH

SKILLS Consonants, Vowels, Sight Words.

MATERIALS Four copies of each flash card. At least fifty-two cards for three or four players will be needed.

SUGGESTED ACTIVITY This game is played most effectively with three or more players. Shuffle and deal out seven cards to each player, putting the remaining cards face down in the center of the table. Each player first checks his hand for possible pairs which, if any, are placed in front of him. The game begins with the dealer who asks the person on his right for a particular word. For example, "Give me all of your cards that say cat." If that player does not have any cat cards, he says "Go fish." Player one then draws one card from the stack and the game progresses to player two. The object is to collect pairs which are then placed in front of each player. The first player to get rid of his cards is the winner. Note: Letters or numbers may be used on the flash cards instead of words. A deck of playing cards may be used for number practice.

ALPHABET TRAIN

SKILLS **Fine Motor, Visual Motor.**

MATERIALS Oaktag, poster board or heavy construction paper, magic marker.

DIRECTIONS Cut one 80″ by 3″ strip of poster paper. The pieces of paper may need to be spliced together. Using the magic marker, write the letters of the alphabet along the strip, approximately one letter for every three inches. Now cut between each letter following a curved or zig zag pattern to form a puzzle edge. Make certain that each cut is a different puzzle edge. See the diagram. Use a dark colored magic marker to frame around each puzzle piece after they have been cut. Laminate or use clear contact paper to protect the pieces.

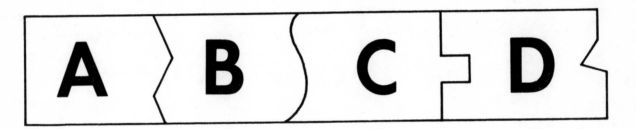

SUGGESTED ACTIVITIES

1. Spread the puzzle parts on the floor. The child can then match puzzle pieces together to form the *Alphabet Train*.

2. Make two sets of puzzle pieces and two children can play together, seeing who can assemble his alphabet train first.

SECTION TWO

MATHEMATICS

MATHEMATICS CHECKLIST

LEARNING APTITUDES

ACTIVITY/GAME		Auditory			Visual					Response Required	
		Auditory Reception*	Auditory Association*	Auditory Memory*	Visual Reception*	Visual Association*	Visual Memory*	Visual Discrimination*	Visual Sequencing*	Verbal Response*	Manual Response*
Deck of Cards	p. 60	✓	✓	✓+	✓	✓+	✓	✓+	✓	✓	✓
Estimating	p. 62	✓			✓	✓	✓			✓	✓
Number Disc Board	p. 64	✓	✓	✓+	✓	✓	✓+	✓+	✓+		✓
Operation Cover-Up	p. 66				✓	✓		✓			✓
Fishing	p. 68				✓	✓				✓	
Egg Carton Toss	p. 69				✓			✓		✓	✓
Number Maze	p. 70	✓	✓	✓+	✓	✓	✓	✓+			✓
Bean Bag Game	p. 72	✓		✓	✓	✓	✓	✓		✓	✓
Partner Practice	p. 74	✓	✓	✓+						✓	
Cross Out	p. 76				✓	✓	✓				✓
Fact War	p. 78				✓	✓	✓			✓	
Equation Search	p. 79				✓	✓	✓	✓+	✓+	✓	✓
Chip 'N	p. 80				✓	✓+					✓
Road Maps	p. 82	✓	✓	✓+	✓	✓	✓	✓+			✓
Menu Games	p. 83				✓					✓	✓
Money Puzzle	p. 84				✓	✓+					✓
Money Cards	p. 85				✓	✓+	✓	✓			✓
Get Rich	p. 86				✓	✓+	✓	✓+			✓
Clock Puzzle	p. 88				✓	✓+					✓
Measuring Worm	p. 89				✓	✓					✓
Equals	p. 90				✓	✓	✓	✓+	✓		✓
Wooden Math Cubes	p. 93	✓	✓	✓+	✓	✓	✓	✓+	✓	✓	✓
Pit Stop	p. 94				✓	✓	✓	✓		✓	✓
Try-A-Triangle	p. 96				✓	✓	✓	✓+		✓	

✓+ Primary Emphasis of Activity
✓ Involved but not Primary
* Defined in Appendix

| | MATHEMATICS SKILLS | | | | | | | Operations | | | | Practical Application | | | | MOTOR SKILLS | | | | |
Numbers and Numeration	Matching	Equality	Counting	Place Value	Fractions	Decimals	Addition	Subtraction	Multiplication	Division	Money	Time	Measurement	Problem Solving	Gross Motor*	Fine Motor*	Visual Motor*	Appropriate for Secondary*	Easily Adapted for Secondary*
√+	√+	√	√+	√+			√+	√+	√+	√+								√	√
√			√		√		√	√					√+	√+	√	√	√	√	√
√+			√+				√	√	√	√						√	√		
√							√+	√+	√+	√+				√+		√	√	√	
√							√+	√+	√+	√+	√+	√+			√		√		
√							√+	√+	√+	√+						√+	√+		
√+								√	√	√						√	√		
√							√+	√+	√+	√+					√+	√	√+		
√							√+	√+	√+	√+								√	
√		√+					√+	√+						√+		√	√	√	
√		√					√+	√+	√+	√+								√	√
√		√+					√+	√+											√
√		√+					√							√+					√
√							√+	√+					√+	√+		√	√	√	√
√							√+	√+			√+			√				√	√
√	√+	√					√+				√+					√	√		
√	√+	√	√				√+				√+								
√		√					√+				√+			√+		√	√		
√	√+											√+				√	√		
√					√								√+			√	√		
√		√+			√	√	√+	√+						√+			√	√	
√		√		√+			√+	√+	√+	√+							√	√	√
√		√					√+	√+	√+	√+							√	√	
√		√					√+	√+	√+	√+								√	

DECK OF CARDS

SKILLS
Numbers and Numeration, Matching, Counting, Place Value, Addition, Subtraction, Multiplication, Division, Equality.

MATERIALS
Regulation deck of cards with jokers and face cards removed.

SUGGESTED ACTIVITIES
A deck of cards can be used for a variety of math drills and games, ranging from beginning math readiness to multiplication/division practice. The number cards help to reinforce the numeral/quantity association. The following are activities that may be used with playing cards.

1. Students can practice sorting, matching, numeral identification and counting activities. Have the student match suits, all fours, all sixes, etc., together. Have the student count shapes on the cards or sequence cards in numerical order by suit, etc.

 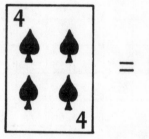 = 2 4

2. Students can practice reading composite numbers formed by placing two or more cards side by side as in the diagram. Have the student practice reading and writing the number of two or more cards together.

3. Students can practice concepts of more than and less than. Have a student pick a card and identify the numeral. Then have him find another card that is "more than" or greater than the first card and a card that is "less than" or fewer than the first card.

4. A card deck is useful for activities such as finding equations. Use any of the four math operations. Call out, "Find two numbers, when added together, equal seven." If every student in the group has his own deck, you can easily check to see who knows the combinations. Make it a visual activity by writing the answer on the board.

5. Deal all students three cards, have them sort their three cards in any order forming a composite number from all three. The student

DECK OF CARDS

that is able to form the largest number (e.g., 342) wins all the cards dealt to all players. Two or four cards could be dealt for practice with tens, thousands, etc.

6. Students can work in pairs for basic drill in the operations of addition and multiplication. A graph should be used as illustrated. One student should know the facts being practiced (such as the multiplication facts). One card is drawn which becomes the constant for operations (e.g., if a 3 is drawn then the constant is 3x). The student then draws the top card which is the number that 3 is multiplied by. The partner marks a space in the graph each time a correct answer is given as illustrated. After working completely through the deck each specific pair has been practiced four times with a graph showing where the strong combinations are and where additional practice is needed because errors have been made.

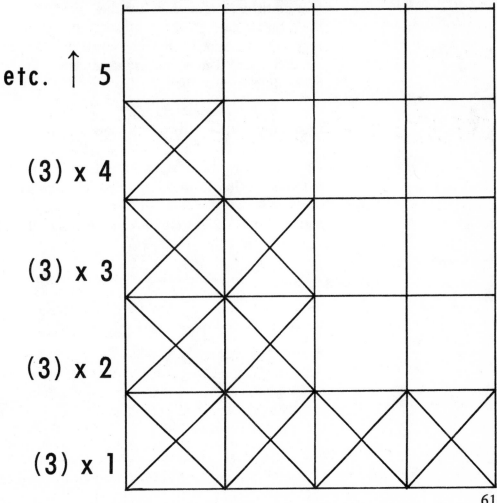

ESTIMATING

SKILLS
Measurement, Problem Solving, Numbers and Numeration, Counting, Fractions, Addition, Subtraction, Gross Motor, Fine Motor, Visual Motor.

MATERIALS
Estimating card as illustrated in the diagram. Other materials are variable depending on specific activity.

SUGGESTED ACTIVITIES
Many students have difficulty with being able to make a "good" (accurate) estimate. Estimating often involves measuring and provides meaningful practice of this skill.

1. *Estimate*: How tall or high? How far or how wide?
   Penny Pitch: Each student pitches his penny against a wall. All players then estimate how far their penny is from the wall, using the estimate card. See the illustration. After estimates are made, they each measure to find the actual distance and subtract to find the difference. The winner is the student with the lowest total score in the difference column.

2. *Other things to estimate*:
   Liquid quantities: How many pints or cups of water in the can?

   Objects: How many beans/buttons in the jar? How many chairs in the auditorium?

   Sums: 4380 + 2463 (involves rounding to the nearest 100).

ESTIMATING

Name		
Estimate	Actual	Difference

ESTIMATING CARD

NUMBER DISC BOARD

SKILLS Numbers and Numeration, Counting, Addition, Subtraction, Multiplication, Division, Fine Motor, Visual Motor.

MATERIALS Poster board or plywood, magic marker, 100 small nails or curtain hooks.

DIRECTIONS Mark the posterboard or plywood off into a grid with ten squares to a side as in the diagram. If you are using plywood, drive a small nail into the center of each square. If poster board is being used, insert a curtain hook through the center of each hole in such a manner that small discs can be hung on them when the grid board is standing upright or in a vertical position leaning against a chair. Number discs can either be made by cutting small circles of oaktag or purchased at a school supply outlet. Each disc will have to have a small hole in it such that it can be hung on the nails in the grid. A total of 100 discs will be needed. The discs should be numbered from 1 to 100.

SUGGESTED ACTIVITIES

1. The child can place the tags on the boards in the proper sequence for number (counting) practice.

2. With all discs in place on the board, twenty-five or thirty can be removed randomly. These may then be mixed into a pile and the child's task is to replace them in their appropriate position.

3. This board can be used for a variety of math operations. For example, the teacher calls out 2 x 2 and the child retrieves disc number four as the answer. This can be done individually or as a small group activity with the first child retrieving the correct disc being permitted to keep it.

4. With all discs in place have the child remove all even (or odd) numbered discs. Or the child may remove all discs that are multiples of a certain number or all discs that can be divided by a certain number.

5. Number disc boards are also useful for practice on counting by 10's or 5's, etc.

NUMBER DISC BOARD

OPERATION COVER UP

SKILLS   Addition, Subtraction, Multiplication, Division, Problem Solving, Numbers and Numeration, Fine Motor, Visual Motor.

MATERIALS   Magic markers, oaktag, three dice, fifty position markers (beans, chips, etc.).

DIRECTIONS   Cut an 8″ by 8″ square of oaktag for the game board. Divide it into sixty-four squares. See the diagram. Put the numbers shown on the diagram in the same places on the game board.

SUGGESTED ACTIVITY   Two or more children can play this game. Each player has one roll per turn with the dice. The first player rolls the three dice. He must use one or two operations with the three numbers revealed by the dice. That number is then covered with a position marker on the game board. For example, if player one rolled a 3, a 5, and a 4, he would have several options—he might add 3 and 5 and multiply by 4 giving him 32 to cover on the game board—or—he might multiply 3 times 5 and subtract 4 giving him 11 to cover on the game board. Player one covers his number and cannot score on his first turn. Subsequent players continue in the same fashion. In order to score in this game, players must cover a number on the board which is adjacent to another covered number either vertically, horizontally, or diagonally. A player scores one point for each adjacent covered number.

If a player is unable to compute a number which has not already been covered, he loses his turn and the game progresses on to the next player. After a designated period of time, the player with the highest score is the winner. An egg timer may be used to limit the amount of time a player may take on any one turn.

OPERATION COVER UP

OPERATION COVER-UP

1	2	3	4	5	6	7	8
9	10	11	12	13	14	15	16
17	18	19	20	21	22	23	24
25	26	27	28	29	30	31	32
33	34	35	36	37	38	39	40
41	42	44	45	48	50	54	55
60	64	66	72	75	80	90	96
100	108	120	125	144	150	180	216

FISHING

SKILLS Addition, Subtraction, Multiplication, Division, Money, Time, Numbers and Numeration, Gross Motor, Visual Motor.

MATERIALS Stick or wooden dowel approximately three feet long, with a three-foot string attached to one end (fishing pole) and a small magnet for a "hook," paperclips, marking pen and construction paper.

DIRECTIONS Cut fish from construction paper and put paper clips on them. Write addition, subtraction, multiplication or division facts on each fish.

SUGGESTED ACTIVITIES

1. Designate an area (circle on the floor or behind a divider) as a fishing pond. The students take turns fishing, and may keep the fish they catch if they can correctly answer the math fact. Fish are caught when the magnet makes contact with the paper clip on a fish. The fisherman with the highest total after all the fish are caught is the winner.

2. Write words to be studied on each fish.

3. Draw clocks on each fish and the fisherman must read the time correctly.

4. Glue "money" (cut from workbooks) on each fish. If the fisherman counts the money on the fish correctly, he keeps the fish.

EGG CARTON TOSS

SKILLS Addition, Subtraction, Multiplication, Division, Numbers and Numeration, Fine Motor, Visual Motor.

MATERIALS Egg cartons, egg trays or large muffin tin, marking pen, buttons or beans to toss.

DIRECTIONS Use the marking pen to write a number from 1 to 9 in the bottom of each cup.

SUGGESTED ACTIVITIES

1. Taking turns each student tosses two buttons into two cups. He adds, subtracts, multiplies or divides the numbers in the bottom of each cup. If he performs the operation correctly and says the right answer, he then receives that many points. For example, the buttons land in 2 and 4. If the task is to add, the student adds 2 and 4 which equals 6. Six points are then added to his score. After a designated period of time (e.g., ten minutes) or number of trials (e.g., eight trials) the student with the highest score is the winner.

2. Write letters in the bottom of the cups. Taking turns each student tosses six buttons into any of the cups. Using the six letters he writes as many words as he can spell in sixty seconds. At the end of the time period the student with the most words spelled correctly is the winner.

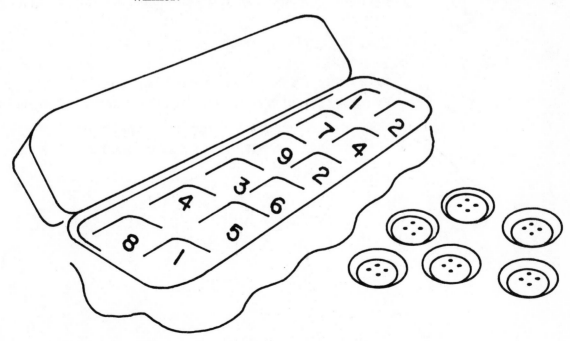

69

NUMBER MAZE

SKILLS Numbers and Numeration, Subtraction, Multiplication, Division, Fine Motor, Visual Motor.

MATERIALS Ditto master, primer typewriter.

DIRECTIONS Type numbers in any random order on a ditto master similar to the example. Type approximately fifteen numbers across and fifteen numbers down. Double space between numbers on a line, and single space between rows.

SUGGESTED ACTIVITIES The following ideas will illustrate a few ways to use Number Maze.

1. Dictate a problem and have the child circle the answer on his Number Maze.

2. Have the child circle all of the even numbers, or all of the odd numbers, or numbers that can be divided into certain numbers, etc.

3. Have the child connect certain numbers with a straight line. For example, "Connect two numbers that when added together, equal sixteen."

4. Have the child use his Number Maze as an answer sheet for a worksheet of addition or subtraction facts. Answers may even be color coded for easy correction. For example, "Circle the answer to number one in red; circle the answer to number two in blue, etc."

5. Have the child make geometric shapes on top of the Number Maze. For example, "Draw a triangle connecting a 6, a 4, and a 6."

NUMBER MAZE

NUMBER MAZE

```
2  9  7  5  8  1  4  6  8  3  2  8  9  7  3
5  8  3  2  9  1  7  5  4  2  9  6  5  2  1
3  5  7  9  1  2  4  6  7  9  4  3  2  1  9
9  8  6  3  2  4  6  9  1  6  8  5  4  9  2
1  9  6  3  2  6  8  7  4  3  6  0  9  7  8
8  7  4  9  4  2  7  3  9  5  7  4  1  5  4
7  6  3  9  6  2  4  6  8  6  3  1  9  7  4
5  4  7  8  9  4  3  2  1  7  5  9  4  7  2
7  9  8  4  6  8  3  9  1  7  2  9  7  4  8
0  7  5  9  3  1  5  2  4  8  7  4  6  3  9
4  8  6  9  3  2  8  9  1  7  6  5  7  9  1
9  7  5  3  9  1  7  4  2  6  3  8  5  9  3
3  2  5  7  8  9  5  7  4  9  1  4  7  3  2
6  4  6  9  1  2  4  3  7  5  9  1  7  6  4
1  9  3  2  9  1  7  5  6  1  2  1  8  6  3
```

71

BEAN BAG GAME

SKILLS   Addition, Subtraction, Multiplication, Division, Numbers and Numeration, Gross Motor, Fine Motor, Visual Motor.

MATERIALS   Bean bags, flash cards, large cardboard box or plywood board with stand, thumb tacks.

DIRECTIONS   The target surface will either be the bottom of the cardboard box or the plywood board depending on which is used. This target surface will be in a vertical position facing the child as in the illustration. Cut any number of holes in the target surface large enough for a bean bag to pass through easily with some clearance. Place either numbers or words on the flash cards. Secure cards above each hole with thumb tacks. See the illustration.

BEAN BAG GAME

SUGGESTED ACTIVITIES

1. *Number Throw*. Mark a foul line on the floor several feet from the board. Pin numbers above each hole. The children take turns throwing the bean bag through the holes with each child taking three throws per turn. The task is to perform the math operation (e.g., addition, subtraction, etc.) that is being practiced, using the numbers over the holes which are hit. For example, suppose he gets a 3 and a 5. If the game is *add*, his score for the first round is 8. If the game is *multiply*, his score would be 15, or 2 if the game is *subtraction*. Scores are kept on a separate sheet of paper and the child with the highest score at the end of the game is the winner.

2. *Word Throw*. Play as described in number throw but pin words above each hole. Taking turns, the children try to collect words by throwing the bean bag through the hole (one throw per turn). The teacher may call out the word to be hit or the children may choose the word they wish to hit. When a child makes a shot he reads the word, and if correct, removes it. At the end of the time period the child with the most words is the winner. When a word is removed from the game board, other cards may be added.

PARTNER PRACTICE

SKILLS Addition, Subtraction, Multiplication, Division, Numbers and Numeration.

MATERIALS Partner practice sheet (see the illustration), a tape recording with a beep at ten second intervals.

DIRECTIONS Partner one holds partner two's drill sheet and calls out the fact problems individually for two to answer. One records the answer given by two in the space next to the problem. Two must respond in ten seconds (taped beep signal). When the drill is finished two then checks his sheet to see which problems he has missed. He can make his own practice flash cards to help him learn the facts he has missed.

SUGGESTED ACTIVITY This activity can be used with any of the basic fact combinations. The tape recorder is to run continually throughout this exercise. Ten seconds gives a child enough time to answer and enough time for the first child to record the second child's answer.

PARTNER PRACTICE

TIMES TABLE DRILL—PARTNER PRACTICE—6's

Test Record: Student:
   1.   Date Started:
   2.   Date Passed:
   3.

	Date								
6 x 10 =	60								
6 x 4 =	24								
6 x 9 =	54								
6 x 7 =	42								
6 x 6 =	36								
6 x 2 =	12								
6 x 8 =	48								
6 x 5 =	30								
6 x 9 =	54								
6 x 10 =	60								
6 x 7 =	42								
6 x 8 =	48								
6 x 6 =	36								
6 x 0 =	0								
6 x 5 =	30								
6 x 1 =	6								
6 x 2 =	12								

CROSS OUT

SKILLS   Equality, Addition, Subtraction, Problem Solving, Numbers and Numeration, Fine Motor, Visual Motor.

MATERIALS   Poster board, magic marker, dice, grease pencil or crayon.

DIRECTIONS   Cut a rectangle out of poster board approximately 10″ x 6″ or larger. Divide it into nine sections on each side of a center line using a magic marker. See the example. Laminate or cover it with clear contact paper.

CROSS OUT

Player 1	Player 2
1	9
2	8
3	7
4	6
5	5
6	4
7	3
8	2
9	1
Total:	Total:

CROSS OUT

1. Two children play together, facing each other with the board placed between them. The first player shakes the dice. He then crosses out the appropriate numbers on his side of the board. For example, if he shakes a 5 and a 3, he would have the following options:

    a. crossing out the 5 and the 3
        OR
    b. crossing out any numbers that equal 8
        (4, 3, and 1; 6 and 2; 7 and 1, etc.)

    The players take turns throwing the dice and crossing out numbers on their side of the board. The first player to cross out all of his numbers automatically wins. Numbers can only be crossed out once. The game may also end when players have no cross out options open to them. Each player then adds up his remaining numbers that have not been crossed out and the child with the lowest score is the winner. This game involves a fair amount of strategy and is excellent for drill on simple addition facts.

2. By changing the numbers on the board, and using one die, this game may be used for subtraction practice. For example, players would cross out the two numbers that, when subtracted, would equal the number indicated on the die. If the number rolled was 3, the player could cross out 6 and 3, or 5 and 2, or 8 and 5, etc.

FACT WAR

SKILLS   Addition, Subtraction, Multiplication, Division, Numbers and Numeration, Equality.

MATERIALS   276 cards approximately 2½″ by 4″, magic marker.

DIRECTIONS   Forty-four cards with the addition facts through 10 will be needed for game one.

Fifty-two cards with the subtraction facts through 10 will be neded for game two.

Sixty cards, some with addition and some with subtraction facts through 10 will be needed for game three.

Fifty-six cards with the multiplication facts through 100 will be needed for game four.

Sixty-four cards with the division facts through the product of 81 will be needed for game five.

SUGGESTED ACTIVITIES

1. This game is played best with an even number of children. After the cards have been shuffled, deal face down, the same number of cards to each child. Without looking at their pile of cards, each player turns the top card over on the signal "War!" The teacher or the leader may call out the signal. The first child to answer the problem on his card correctly out loud takes everyone's face up card.

    If a tie occurs, each player, on the signal, turns over the next card. The player who has collected the most cards at the end of the game is the winner.

    This procedure can be used for games one through five, using the addition, subtraction, multiplication and division set of cards.

2. Play as described in number one, but the player whose card has the highest value collects all the cards.

EQUATION SEARCH

SKILLS Equality, Addition, Subtraction, Numbers and Numeration.

MATERIALS Sixty-five oak tag cards.

DIRECTIONS Write the following on the cards:

      six cards with red plus signs
      seven cards with green minus signs
      thirteen cards with blue equal signs
      five with 1's
      five with 2's
      five with 3's
      four with 4's
      four with 5's
      four with 6's
      three with 7's
      three with 8's
      three with 9's
      three with 0's.

SUGGESTED ACTIVITY This game may be used with two or more players. Place all of the cards face down on the table. Players take turns picking one card at a time and turning it face up. Cards are then left face up. When a player sees an equation he calls out, "Equation!" He must then say the equation correctly before placing it in sequence in front of him (e.g., "Five plus three equals eight"). The winner is the player who finds the most equations.

CHIP 'N

SKILLS Equality, Problem Solving, Numbers and Numeration, Addition.

MATERIALS Oaktag, magic markers, poker chips or colored circles to match colors on the game boards, one die.

DIRECTIONS Make a 9″ by 12″ board for each player divided into four sections. Each section should be a different color. See the example:

WHITE	RED	BLUE	YELLOW

Each child should also have a value card. See the example:

Value of Chips
4 whites = 1 red
4 reds = 1 blue
4 blues = 1 yellow
4 yellows = the winner

CHIP 'N

SUGGESTED ACTIVITIES

1. This game needs two or more players and a banker. The object of the game is to obtain four yellow chips. This is done by trading with the banker. The banker handles all chips and deals them out to the players according to the number on the die thrown by the player. For example, if a player throws a six he is given six white chips by the banker. The player can then trade in four white chips for one red chip. The chips are kept on each player's board according to color. The first player to obtain four yellow chips is the winner.

2. Use other values on the value cards.

3. Use two dice and add them.

ROAD MAPS

SKILLS   Addition, Subtraction, Measurement, Problem Solving, Numbers and Numeration, Fine Motor, Visual Motor.

MATERIALS   State road maps, area maps, etc.

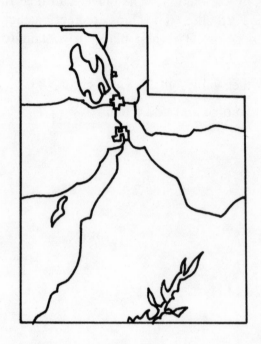

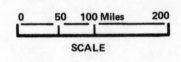

SCALE

DIRECTIONS   Laminate or cover with clear contact paper.

SUGGESTED ACTIVITIES

1. Have the child locate and circle certain places on the map. For example, "Find and circle Smithville."

2. Give the children map coordinates and have them find the nearest city.

3. Give two locations, and have the child compute the mileage.

4. Have the children estimate distances, and then figure the actual distance.

5. Give the children two routes to a particular location and have them find the shortest route.

82

MENU GAMES

SKILLS   Addition, Subtraction, Money, Numbers and Numeration, Problem Solving.

MATERIALS   Collect a variety of menus from restaurants.

SUGGESTED ACTIVITIES

1. Children can take turns ordering items or meals and totaling the amount.

2. Children can be given a certain amount of money, order items, and then figure the change they should receive from the cashier.

3. Children can order items and then estimate their cost. Then, have the children figure their actual bill and find the difference.

4. In a group situation, see who can order a complete dinner (entree, dessert, drink) for the least amount, or see who can spend the closest to $5.00 without going over.

MONEY PUZZLE

SKILLS   Matching, Addition, Money, Numbers and Numeration, Equality, Fine Motor, Visual Motor.

MATERIALS   Oaktag, marking pen, pictures of coins cut from workbooks.

DIRECTIONS Cut the oaktag into a set of 3" x 5" cards. On the top half of each card glue on some of the coins. Write the amount the coins are worth on the bottom half of each card. Then cut the cards into two puzzle pieces (see the illustration).

SUGGESTED ACTIVITY This is an independent, self-correcting activity. The child puts the puzzles together by correctly matching the coins with the amounts.

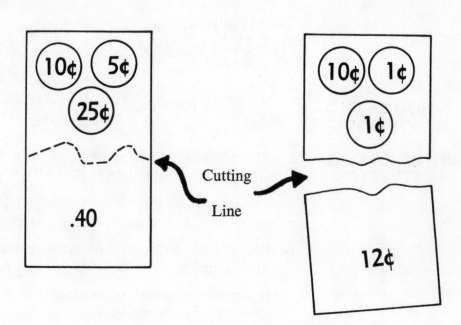

MONEY CARDS

SKILLS   Matching, Addition, Money, Numbers and Numeration, Equality, Counting.

MATERIALS   2½″ x 4″ oaktag cards, magic marker, pictures of coins and bills or use play money or real money.

DIRECTIONS   Write an amount of money on each card. See the example. Cards can be made according to the student's skill level. For example, one group could be amounts below $0.50, or amounts above $0.50, and so forth.

Example:

$$\boxed{\$0.45}$$

SUGGESTED ACTIVITIES

1. The child draws a card and counts out that amount of money.

2. One child draws a card. The player who can make that amount using the least number of coins keeps the card. The player with the most cards at the end of the game is the winner.

GET RICH

SKILLS Addition, Money, Problem Solving, Numbers and Numeration, Equality, Fine Motor, Visual Motor.

MATERIALS Oaktag, one die, construction paper.

DIRECTIONS Make a game board 9" x 12" similar to the illustration. Cut forty colored circles (one color for each player) out of construction paper. These are to be used as markers.

SUGGESTED ACTIVITIES Throw the die to see who goes first. The player with the highest number starts. Each time the die is thrown the player wins coins from the board. The player shows which coins have been won by covering them with their colored circles. The number shown on the die tells how much money can be covered. See the illustration. A player can use any combination of coins to cover the amount needed unless a six is thrown. The first player to get a six can cover the dollar bill. If a player cannot cover the exact amount needed, the turn is lost. When all the money is covered, players add up the amounts of the coins they have covered to find out who is the winner.

GET RICH

GET RICH

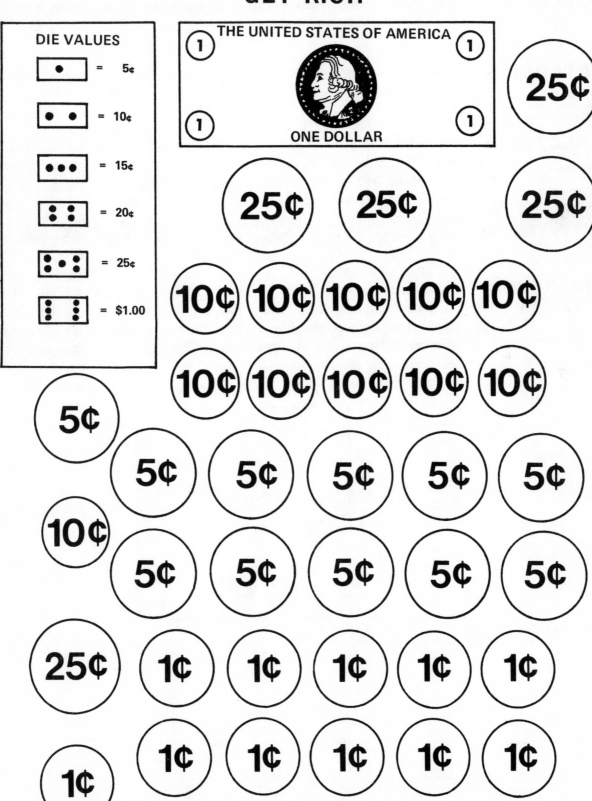

DIE VALUES

•	=	5¢
• •	=	10¢
• • •	=	15¢
• •	=	20¢
• • •	=	25¢
• • •	=	$1.00

THE UNITED STATES OF AMERICA
1 1
1 1
ONE DOLLAR

25¢

25¢   25¢   25¢

10¢ 10¢ 10¢ 10¢ 10¢

10¢ 10¢ 10¢ 10¢ 10¢

5¢

5¢   5¢   5¢   5¢   5¢

10¢   5¢   5¢   5¢   5¢   5¢

25¢   1¢   1¢   1¢   1¢   1¢

1¢   1¢   1¢   1¢   1¢   1¢

87

CLOCK PUZZLE

SKILLS Matching, Time, Numbers and Numeration, Fine Motor, Visual Motor.

MATERIALS Construction paper, magic marker. Laminate cards or use clear contact paper to preserve them.

DIRECTIONS Cut construction paper into rectangles approximately 4" by 5". Take one of the cards and draw a clock on the top half. See the illustration. On the bottom half of the card write the time indicated by the hands of the clock. Now cut the two portions apart following a curved or zig-zag pattern, forming a puzzle edge. Follow this same procedure with several cards each with a different time and puzzle edge.

SUGGESTED ACTIVITY Spread the puzzle parts from several puzzles on the table or floor. The child then can match the appropriate clock faces to the written time statements. Because the puzzle edges are cut differently, only the parts with correct time and pictures will fit. This can be an independent, self-correcting activity.

Example   Cutting line

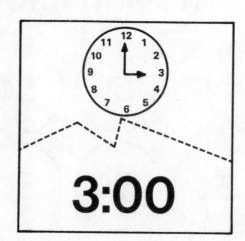

3:00

MEASURING WORM

SKILLS
Measurement, Numbers and Numeration, Fractions, Fine Motor, Visual Motor.

MATERIALS
Construction paper, a cube of wood for die (or cover a regular die with masking tape), scissors, rulers, scotch tape.

DIRECTIONS
Take a portion of the construction paper and make a worm head similar to the illustration for each child who is to play. The remaining part of the construction paper should be cut into long strips. Label the die according to the number of inches the children are going to measure. The die could have whole numbers, fractions, etc. printed on it, depending on the childrens' skill level. Each child should have a worm head, ruler, scissors and strips of paper.

SUGGESTED ACTIVITIES

1. The first player rolls the die. He then measures and cuts the number of inches indicated on the die from a paper strip and attaches it to the worm head. This continues until one child's worm measures twenty inches or whatever length has been designated.

2. Begin this game by giving each child a strip of paper the same length. For example, each child may have a thirty inch worm behind his worm head. Taking turns, each child rolls the die. The number that appears indicates the amount that should be cut off his worm. The winner is the child who is first to cut off his entire worm (or thirty inches). For younger children, put whole numbers on the die.

89

EQUALS

SKILLS

Equality, Addition, Subtraction, Problem Solving, Numbers and Numeration, Fractions, Decimals, Visual Motor.

MATERIALS

Thirteen ¾″ hard wood cubes—sanded. Grease pencil, felt tip markers, oaktag, clear contact paper, cup to hold dice.

DIRECTIONS

Put the suggested whole numbers or decimals or fractions on the thirteen cubes. Construct a board from the oaktag. See the illustration. Cover the board with clear contact paper or laminate.

SUGGESTED ACTIVITIES

1. Two or more children can play Equals. Taking turns, each child shakes all thirteen cubes out on the table. Using the numbers face up on each cube, the child finds math combinations (addition or subtraction) and places them in the boxes on the Equals board. The child must also write in the correct operation sign for each equation. For example: $4 + 3 = 7$. His score is the total number of cubes used correctly, or he may add the right-hand column of boxes for his score. Use a stopwatch (45 seconds) or an egg timer to keep the game moving. If a child does not find a combination after the time has expired, another child may identify the combination and add it to his score. The children keep a tally of their own scores.

Equals—Whole Numbers
Suggested values for faces of whole number cubes:

Cube 1   6, 6, 1, 6, 7, 12
Cube 2   10, 6, 12, 6, 8, 10
Cube 3   0, 2, 14, 3, 4, 7
Cube 4   3, 14, 2, 2, 9, 2
Cube 5   6, 15, 7, 1, 6, 9
Cube 6   3, 3, 15, 12, 7, 11
Cube 7   7, 12, 11, 9, 10, 14
Cube 8   5, 12, 3, 7, 13, 8
Cube 9   4, 8, 9, 5, 8, 2
Cube 10 7, 9, 13, 5, 4, 9
Cube 11 3, 4, 0, 1, 10, 2
Cube 12 10, 6, 5, 7, 4, 12
Cube 13 8, 1, 3, 3, 0, 4

EQUALS

Equals—Decimals

Suggested values for faces of decimal cubes:

Cube 1   .5, 2.75, 1, .75, 4, 3
Cube 2   2.25, 2, 1.25, 2, 1, 2.25
Cube 3   1.5, .75, 2, 1.25, 6, 2.75
Cube 4   1, 4, 1.5, .5, 6, 2
Cube 5   .5, 1.5, .5, 1, 1.25, 2
Cube 6   4, 6, 1.75, 1, 2, 1.25
Cube 7   .75, 6, .5, 4, .25, .5
Cube 8   .5, 3, 2, .75, 0, 5
Cube 9   .75, .25, 1.75, .25, 1, 1.5
Cube 10   .5, 3, 2, 1.75, 0, 5
Cube 11   .75, .25, 1.75, .25, 1, 1.5
Cube 12   0, 1, 1.5, 2, 1.5, 1.75
Cube 13   2, 3, 1, 2, 2.75, 1.25
Cube 14   2.75, 4, 2, 2.75, 1, 0
Cube 15   .25, 0, 1.25, 1.75, 2. 25, 1.5
Cube 16   2.75, 2, 1.5, 1, 1.75, 1.5

Equals—Fractions

Suggested values for faces of fraction cubes:

Cube 1   1, 1, ½, 1, 4, 1½
Cube 2   1½, ¼, 0, 1, ¾, 1½
Cube 3   3, 4, 2, 0, 2, 2½
Cube 4   ½, 3, 1½, 2, 1, 4
Cube 5   6, 4, 1, 4, ¾, ¼
Cube 6   2¼, 1, 2, 0, 2½, 6
Cube 7   ¼, 1, 2, ½ ¾, ¼, ¾
Cube 8   ¼, 0, ¼, 2, ¾, 0, 8
Cube 9   2, 4, ¾, 1½, 2½, 1½
Cube 10   2, 1, ¾, ¼, 2, 1
Cube 11   ½, 1, ½, ½, 0, 2
Cube 12   4, 2, 8½, 2½, 0, 2¼
Cube 13   6, 1, ½, 2, 2½, ¾
Cube 14   4, 7, 9, 5, 12, 5
Cube 15   ¾, 6, 2½, ½, 2, 1

EQUALS

EQUALS BOARD

$$\square \quad \square \quad = \quad \square$$

$$\square \quad \square \quad = \quad \square$$

$$\square \quad \square \quad = \quad \square$$

$$\square \quad \square \quad = \quad \square$$

$$\square$$

WOODEN MATH CUBES

SKILLS Place Value, Addition, Subtraction, Multiplication, Division, Numbers and Numeration, Equality, Visual Motor.

MATERIALS Felt tip markers, ¾″ hard wood cubes—sanded. To reuse cubes or change the numbers, cover the cubes with masking tape before writing on them.

SUGGESTED ACTIVITIES

1. *Dice Drill*: Put the numbers 0-5 and 4-9 on two cubes. Roll the cubes on the table for oral drill. The children are instructed to add, subtract, multiply, or divide the two numbers facing up on the cubes. The first child to call out the correct answer gets a point. The child with the most points after a designated amount of time is the winner. Note: If dividing, the child calls out the remainder.

2. *Timed Fact Writing*: Put the numbers 0-5 and 4-9 on the two cubes. Each child will need his own set of cubes. The child has five minutes to roll the two dice. He must write the problem and compute as many math facts as he can. Use addition, subtraction, multiplication, or division, depending upon the child's skill level. The student with the most correct answers is the winner.

3. *Place Value*: Put the numbers 0-9 on the sides of two or more cubes. One child rolls the dice and another child, using the face up numbers, arranges them and reads the number. See the illustration. He receives a point if he reads the number correctly and may then take a turn rolling the dice. The activity may be modified having a child make the largest or smallest possible number.

4. *Math Grab*: Write answers to arithmetic facts on the sides of the cubes. Roll the cubes on the table top and call out a problem, for example, 3 x 8. The first child to grab the 24 cube gets a point. Use addition, subtraction, multiplication, or division. This activity can also be used for simple number identification.

PIT STOP

SKILLS Addition, Subtraction, Multiplication, Division, Numbers and Numeration, Equality, Visual Motor.

MATERIALS Oaktag, felt tip markers, sanded ¾″ wooden cube, four position markers or plastic cars.

DIRECTIONS Make a game board approximately 18″ by 14″, similar to the diagram. Cut the remaining oaktag into forty rectangular cards 2½″ by 4″. Write numbers from one to ten on twenty of the cards, to be used in the number card stack. See the game board. Make ten red rally cards and ten green rally cards. On the red rally cards write phrases similar to the following: "flat tire, go back one space," "accident, lose one turn," "out of gas, lose one turn," etc. On the green rally cards, write phrases such as: "avoided accident, go ahead one space," "successful pass, take another turn," etc. Place cards face down in their appropriate stacks on the game board. Number the sides of the wooden cube from one to three.

SUGGESTED ACTIVITIES

1. Two to four children can play this game. Beginning in the pit, the first player rolls the die and moves his marker the designated number of spaces. If he rolls a two, he would land on the four space on the game board. He then takes the top card from the number card stack and adds it to the number four. If his answer is correct he may remain on the square. If it is incorrect he must return to his previous position.

   If a child lands on a red square he draws the top card from the Red Rally Stack and follows the directions written on the card. The same procedure is followed when a child lands on a green square.

2. Play as described in the game above, but use subtraction, multiplication or division.

PIT STOP

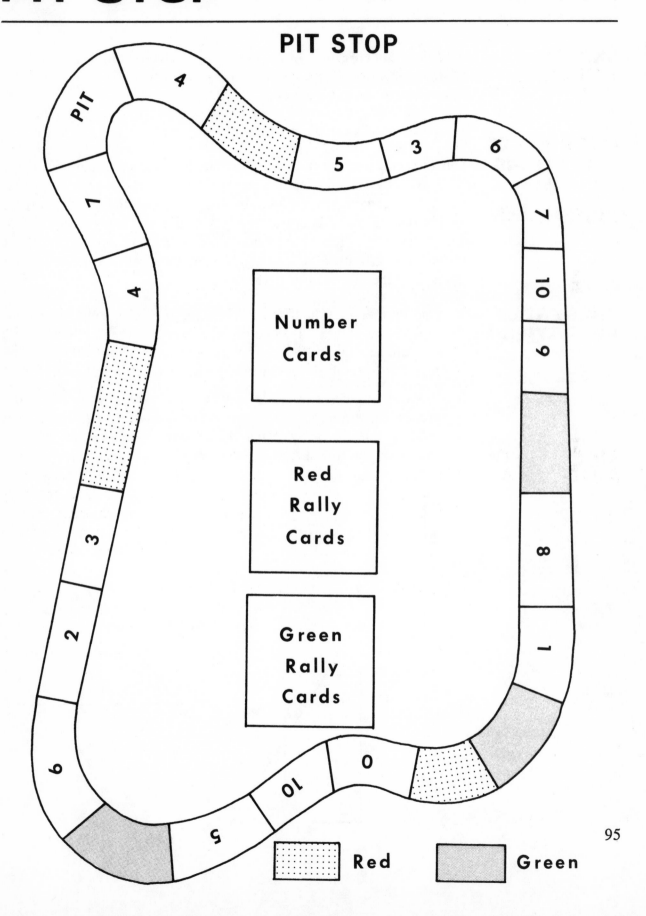

TRY A TRIANGLE

SKILLS Addition, Subtraction, Multiplication, Division, Numbers and Numeration, Equality.

MATERIALS Scraps of tagboard, cardboard or heavy construction paper, laminating equipment or clear contact paper, grease pencil.

DIRECTIONS Cut the scraps of paper into right triangles (see the diagram) about 5″ by 6½″ by 3½″. Different sizes may be preferred for varying situations. Using the magic marker, place digit combinations in the corners as appropriate and the operation signs positioned between the digits. See the diagram. The triangle may then be held on any corner which results in an arithmetic problem to be computed with the answer being covered by the thumb holding the corner.

SUGGESTED ACTIVITIES

1. One partner may hold the triangle for the other child who is to provide the answer. If the correct answer is given, he may receive the number of points equal to the answer. The child with the most points at the end of a given time period is the winner.

2. Working in pairs, each child may be timed with a stopwatch while proceeding through a given number of triangle cards. Have each child call out the answer while the partner covers the corners. The child with the fastest time is the winner.

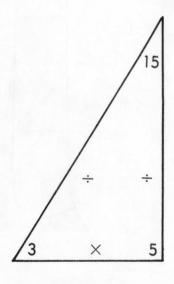
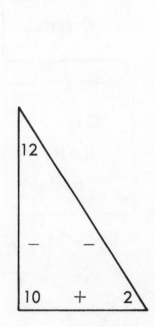
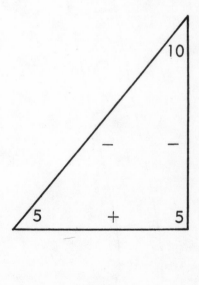

SECTION THREE

GAME BOARDS

SPINNERS

MATERIALS   Poster board or cardboard, plastic from bleach or fabric softener bottles, one screw ½″ in length, two nuts, felt tip pens.

DIRECTIONS   Using a felt tip pen or a magic marker, draw a circle on a piece of poster board. Make the circle at least 6½″ in diameter. Draw pie shaped sections in the circle. See the diagram. Laminate the card or use clear contact paper. Punch a hole in the center of the circle, large enough for the screw. Cut an arrow and a small square, to serve as a washer, out of the plastic. Punch a hole in the arrow and the small square. Place the arrow, nut, and plastic square on the screw. Push the screw through the hole in the card. Thread on the second nut on the underside of the card. Spinners may be mounted on boxes if desired.

SUGGESTED ACTIVITIES

1. Spinners may be used in conjunction with a game board. The child spins the dial to determine the number of spaces he should move a marker.

2. Numbers, words, sounds, or letters to be studied may be written in the spaces. The child spins the dial and must first say the correct word, sound, etc. before moving the indicated number of spaces.

3. For writing practice, the child may spin and write the word or letter. This is especially good for cursive writing practice. Write the words on the spinner in manuscript. The children spin a word and convert it into cursive on their paper. A group of children can play a cursive speed game.

4. For math practice, write numbers, answers, or problems on the spinner. The child must give the correct answer or combination before moving on a game board.

WIZARD WALK

MATERIALS   Poster board, magic markers, laminating equipment or clear contact paper, space marker for students to move to positions, spinner (directions found on page 99).

DIRECTIONS   Look at the sample diagram and then construct a game board similar to Wizard Walk. Laminate the board or cover it with clear contact paper.

SUGGESTED ACTIVITIES

1. Write words, sounds, math facts, etc. to be studied on the game board spaces. The child spins a number and moves his marker on the game board. He must correctly say the word, sound, etc. that he lands on or go back to his previous space.

2. Play the game as described in number one above but the child must respond with a word that rhymes with, begins like, or ends like the word he lands on.

WIZARD WALK

WIZARD WALK

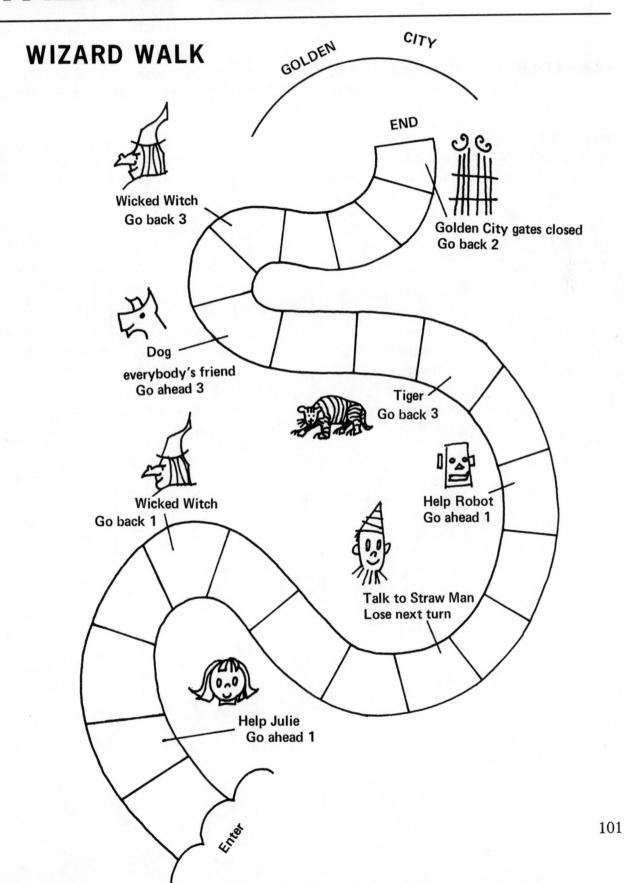

GOLDEN   CITY

END

Wicked Witch
Go back 3

Golden City gates closed
Go back 2

Dog
everybody's friend
Go ahead 3

Tiger
Go back 3

Help Robot
Go ahead 1

Wicked Witch
Go back 1

Talk to Straw Man
Lose next turn

Help Julie
Go ahead 1

Enter

101

FOOTBALL

MATERIALS   Poster board, magic marker, four spinners (directions found on page 99), position markers, laminating equipment or clear contact paper.

DIRECTIONS   Make a football field on the poster board leaving at least six inches extra space behind each goal post (see diagram page 104). Make four spinners, each a different color, which will be attached to the football field. See the diagram.

Write phrases similar to the ones listed below in the pie shaped spaces on each spinner.

Positive Spinner
Field goal—3 points
Touchdown!!!
Forward 5 yards
Forward 10 yards
Pass 5 yards
Run 10 yards
Interception—run 10 yards

Negative Spinner
Penalty—back 10 yards
Stopped—no gain
Fumble
Face Masking—back 15 yards
Clipping—back 15 yards
Off sides—back 5 yards
Holding—back 15 yards
Pass Incomplete

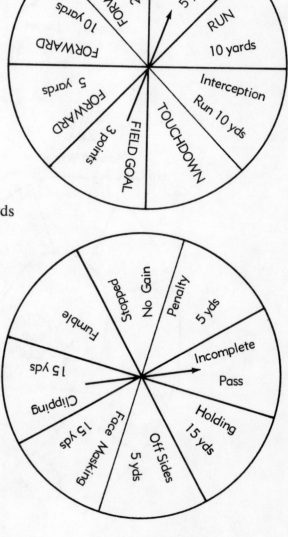

FOOTBALL

Extra Point Kick Spinner
Kick—1 point
Incomplete
Kick—1 point
Incomplete

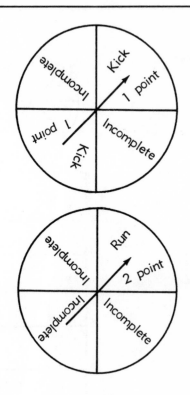

Extra Point Run Spinner
Run—2 points
Incomplete
Incomplete
Incomplete

SUGGESTED ACTIVITIES

Football may be used to add excitement to almost any individual or group activity. It is especially popular with older students. Players begin with their markers placed on the 50 yard line. Regardless of the task, if the child responds correctly, he spins the positive dial and moves his man accordingly on the field. If he responds incorrectly, he spins the negative dial and moves accordingly. When a child makes a touchdown, he has the option to spin the extra point kick dial or the extra point run dial. Each child may keep his own score or children can play in teams.

Flash cards are excellent to use for the tasks when playing football.

FOOTBALL

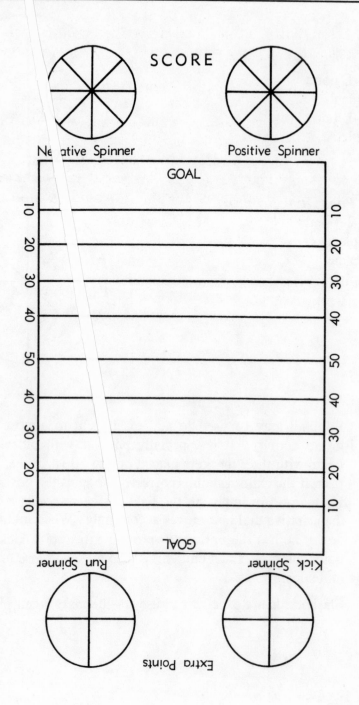

SCORE

Negative Spinner   Positive Spinner

GOAL

10	10
20	20
30	30
40	40
50	50
40	40
30	30
20	20
10	10

GOAL

Run Spinner   Kick Spinner

Extra Points

BASEBALL

MATERIALS Poster board, magic marker, position markers, crayons, laminating equipment or clear contact paper.

DIRECTIONS Make a baseball diamond (any size) for each child.

SUGGESTED ACTIVITY Each child has a baseball diamond, position marker and crayon in front of him during group or individual work. When a child responds correctly he moves a base. Exceptional responses may warrant a double or possibly a home run. The child keeps track of his runs with a crayon mark on the center of the card. Runs can be accumulated weekly or tallied daily.

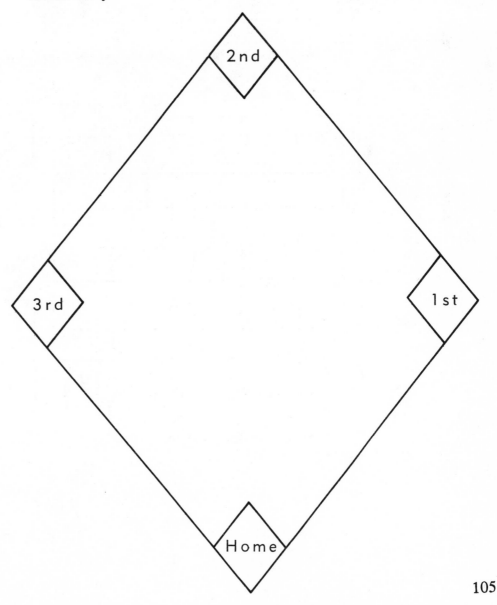

CONCENTRATION

MATERIALS   Twenty-four library pocket cards or envelopes, large poster board, small cards that will fit into the library pockets, magic marker.

DIRECTIONS   Attach the library pockets to the poster board similar to the illustration. Label the pockets with letters on one side and numbers on the other side. See the diagram. A larger or smaller number of pockets may be used depending upon the skill and developmental level of the children. On the cards, to be placed in the pockets, draw or write the appropriate items to be matched in the Concentration game.

CONCENTRATION BOARD

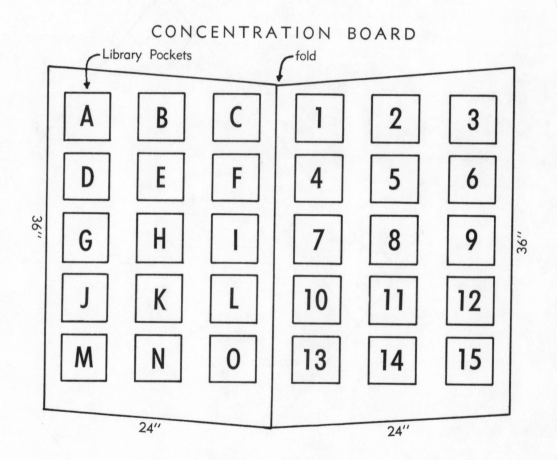

CONCENTRATION

SUGGESTED ACTIVITY

Two or more students may play as in the popular game of concentration. Pairs of cards with the items to be matched are randomly placed in pockets on one side of the board. A student draws one card and attempts to find its match on the other side of the board. If a match is successfully made, the student may keep the cards. A variety of items may be used for matching. Examples include:

  a. Word match, same or rhyming, opposites, etc.
  b. Words and abbreviations.
  c. Color and color word.
  d. Clock face with time (e.g., 4:00 and picture of clock face).
  e. Money amounts, coins with written amounts such as 45¢.
  f. Roman and Arabic numbers (e.g., VI and 6).
  g. Numbers and word (e.g., 4 and four).
  h. Math problems and answers.

TEED OFF

MATERIALS   Poster board, magic markers, four position markers, oaktag.

DIRECTIONS   Using the magic marker, make a game board approximately 36″ x 72″ similar to the golf course diagram (page 110). A larger board with an 18-hole course may be made for older children. Cut 120 flash cards from the oaktag. Divide them into three piles of forty each. Each pile of flash cards will represent a different level of difficulty (i.e. easy, intermediate, difficult) for the material being presented. If desired, these cards can be labeled beginner, amateur, and pro. Math problems, words, letters, etc., may be used as the problems on the flash cards. If a child performs correctly on a problem from the easy or beginner pile he may move ahead one space, two spaces for correct performance on a problem from the intermediate or amateur pile and three spaces for correct performance on one from the difficult or pro pile.

SUGGESTED ACTIVITIES   1. Two to four children may play at the same time. Each child begins by placing their marker in the start space of the first hole. Each child, in turn, then selects a card from either the easy, intermediate, or difficult pile. Correct performance of the problem will allow the child to move ahead the appropriate number of spaces as noted above under directions. If the child does not give a correct response, he stays in the same space. The child may thus determine the number of spaces that can be moved by the difficulty of problems selected. The exception to this is that each child's marker must hit the "green" or putting surface space for every hole. Therefore, if the first hole is a Par 5 the child may initially select a difficult or pro card and if correct, move ahead three spaces. On his next turn, however, the maximum difficulty possible would be an intermediate or amateur problem since there are only two spaces left to the hole. The student may therefore choose a two space card and hit the green or a one space card and wait for the next turn when another one space card would be chosen. The winner is the player who reaches the number nine hole green first.

TEED OFF

2. To add variety, make a fourth stack of cards involving hazards:

> sand trap, back 1 space
> out of bounds, back 2 spaces
> lake, back 1 space
> creek, lose 1 turn
> hit a tree, back 1 space
> hit a fence, lose 1 turn
> lost ball, back 1 space

When a student gives an incorrect response, he then draws one of the hazard cards and follows the instructions written on the card.

3. For older students the game may be altered slightly. They keep track of the spaces moved as "strokes" on a score card for each hole. Under this format, an incorrect response on a three space or pro card would count as three strokes against the player, but the marker would not be moved. A correct response on a pro card would count as one stroke on the score card. The winner would be the student who completes the nine holes with the fewest total strokes.

TEED OFF

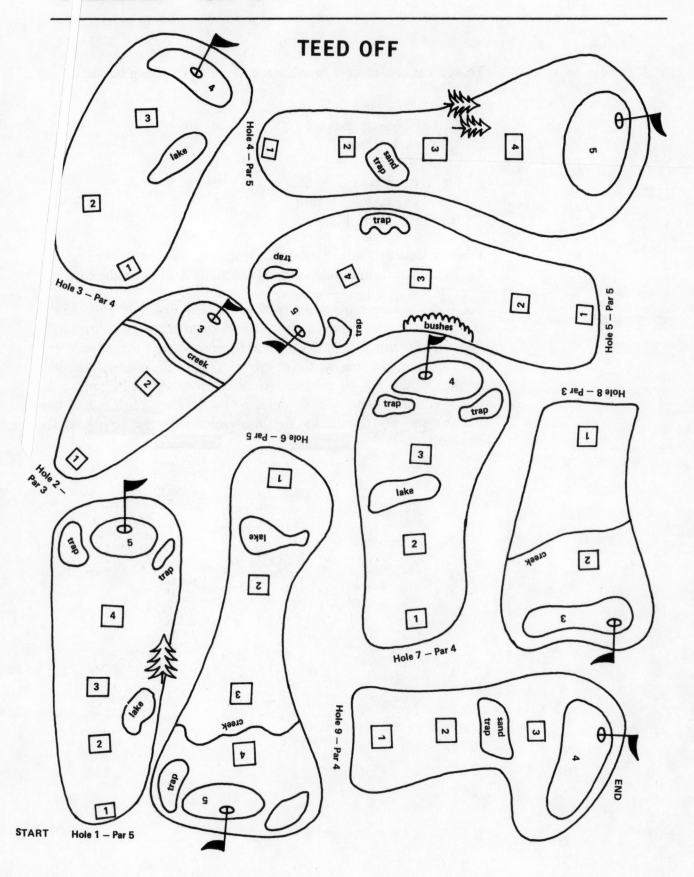

TEED OFF

CHECKERBOARD GAME

MATERIALS   Poster board, magic marker, checkers, grease pencil.

DIRECTIONS   Make a checkerboard—any size, and laminate or cover it with clear contact paper.

SUGGESTED ACTIVITY   Write words, sounds, numbers, etc. that are being studied in the white squares. Play as you would checkers, but the child must say the word, sound, number, etc. before moving to a white square.

HOPSCOTCH

MATERIALS   Poster board, magic markers, flash cards (approximately 3″ x 5″), space markers for students to move to positions, die numbered from 1-6.

DIRECTIONS   Construct a Hopscotch game board (approximately 18″ x 36″) similar to the diagram. Cut flash cards the appropriate size to fit the small squares on the game board.

SUGGESTED ACTIVITIES

1. Write words, sounds, math facts, etc. to be studied on the flash cards. Place one flash card face down on each of the numbered squares (one through ten). Place remaining flash cards face down in a pile aside the game board. Each player begins by placing his position marker on the space labeled Begin. Taking turns, each player rolls the die. The number that appears represents the number of spaces the player moves up on the Hopscotch board. For example, if two comes up, then the child moves two spaces sequentially, and reads the word, sound, etc., that is written on the flash card. If correct, the child leaves the position marker on that space and removes the flash card. A new flash card is then taken from the pile and put in the empty space, face down. If incorrect, the flash card is replaced and the child returns to his previous position. The object of the game is to reach the tenth space as many times as possible in a given time period. Each time a player reaches the tenth space, a point is scored for him. The marker is again placed on Begin and the process is repeated.

2. Play as described above, but start in the number ten space and work backward to number one.

HOPSCOTCH

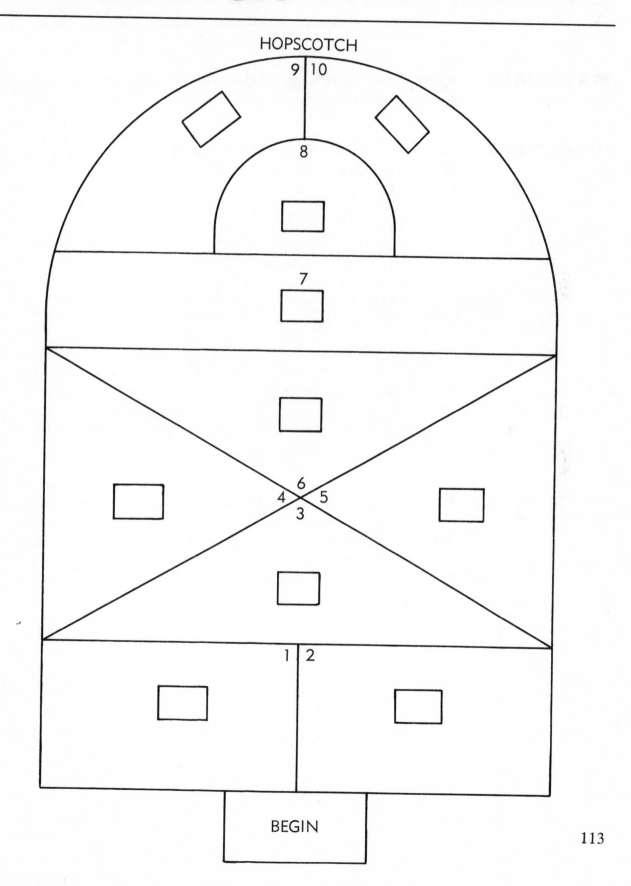

SPLASH DOWN

MATERIALS   Poster board, magic markers, sixty flash cards approximately 3″ x 5″, position markers.

DIRECTIONS   Construct a game board approximately 18″ x 36″ similar to the diagram. Divide the flash cards into three decks; forty cards labeled Task Cards; ten cards labeled A-OK; ten cards labeled Capsule Malfunction. Write words, math facts, letters, etc. on the forty Task Cards. On the *A-OK* cards write sayings, such as:

> On course—move ahead 2 spaces
> Link-up—move ahead 1 space
> Fire Rockets—move ahead 2 spaces
> Successful separation—move ahead 2 spaces.

On the *Capsule Malfunction* cards write sayings such as:

> Space Walk—lose turn
> Course Correction—move back 2 spaces
> 2nd Stage Malfunction—move back 1 space
> Communication Black Out—move back 2 spaces.

SUGGESTED ACTIVITY   Each child begins by placing his position marker on Mission Control. The first player draws the top Task Card. If he responds correctly, he then draws the top A-OK card and follows the directions. If he responds incorrectly to the Task Card, he must draw a Capsule Malfunction card and follow the directions. The first player to Splash Down is the winner of the game.

SPLASH DOWN

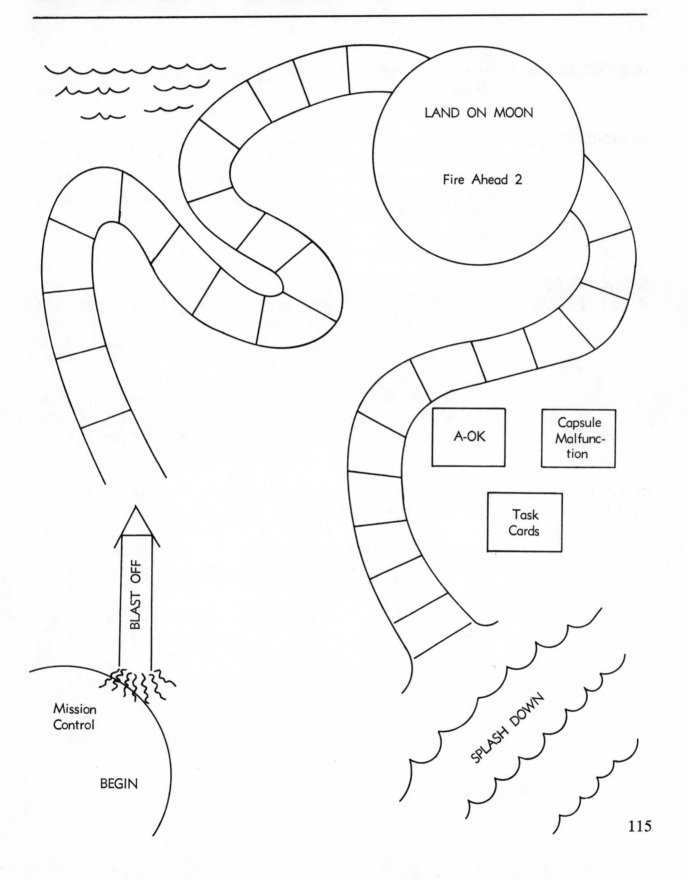

LAND ON MOON

Fire Ahead 2

BLAST OFF

A-OK

Capsule Malfunction

Task Cards

Mission Control

BEGIN

SPLASH DOWN

BIG FOOT

MATERIALS   Poster board, magic markers, dice (one for each player) numbered 1-6, oaktag for task cards.

DIRECTIONS   Cut the poster board into pieces that resemble twenty individual footprints, ten left feet and ten right feet, approximately 18″ by 8″. Cut approximately twenty-five task cards 2½″ x 4″ out of the oaktag. Write words, sounds, arithmetic facts, etc. on the task cards. Each child should have his own die. If desired, one child could be designated as the die roller for the entire group.

SUGGESTED ACTIVITIES

1. Place the feet on the floor in a pattern resembling footprints to make a path. The players start by standing on the beginning footprint. The first player responds to the first task card. It is best to have the teacher or a child read the task card for all the players. If the player answers correctly, he then rolls his die. The number on the die indicates the number of feet he may move ahead. For example, if he rolls a 2 he would move ahead to the second footprint. If the child gives an incorrect response to the task card, he remains in his previous position. The first child to reach the last footprint is the winner.

2. Play as described above but write different sayings on some footprints. For example:

   a. stub toe—lose 1 turn
   b. sprain ankle—go back 2 feet
   c. clean socks—take an extra turn, etc.

3. The feet may be color coded to work on left-right orientation. For example, all of the left feet may be constructed out of red paper and all of the right feet out of blue paper.

BIG FOOT

Big Foot

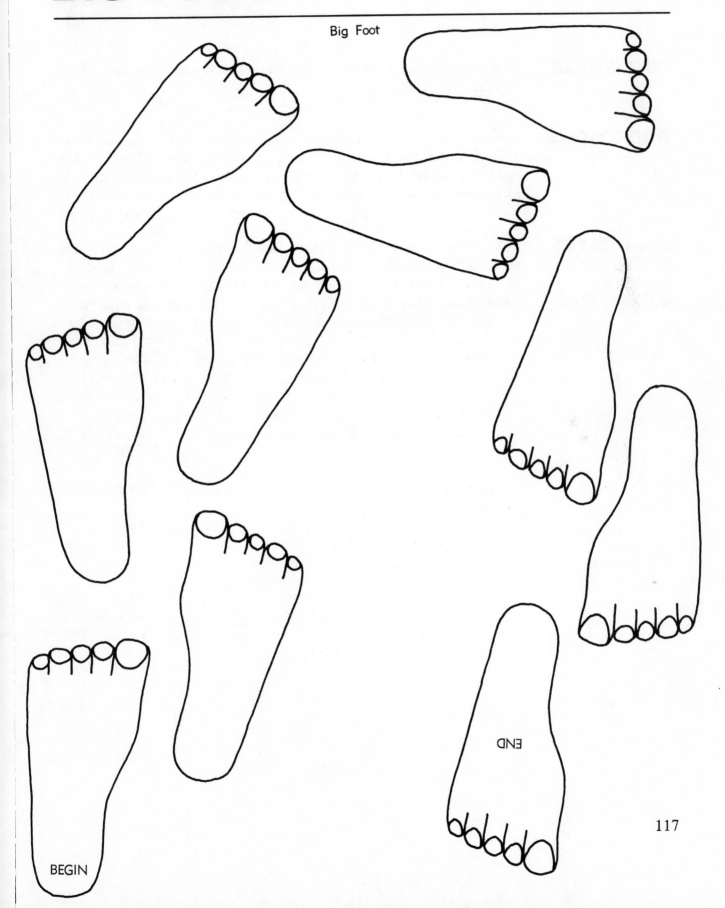

BEGIN

END

SHAPE UP

MATERIALS   Poster board, magic markers, die numbered 1-6, position markers, oak-tag.

DIRECTIONS   Construct a game board similar to the diagram approximately 30″ x 18″. Cut twenty-five task cards out of oaktag. More cards may be needed depending upon the number of players. Write words, sounds, math facts, etc., to be studied on the task cards.

SUGGESTED ACTIVITY   Place the position markers on start. The first player draws the top task card. If he responds correctly, he rolls the die and moves ahead the indicated number of spaces. If he gives an incorrect response, he remains in the same space. The first child to reach the finish line is the winner.

SHAPE UP

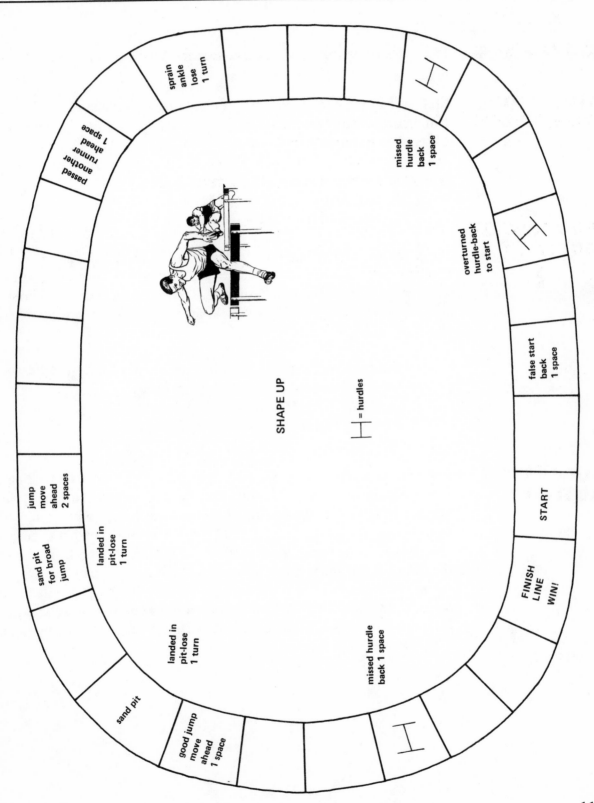

SHAPE UP

H = hurdles

sprain ankle lose 1 turn

passed another runner ahead 1 space

missed hurdle back 1 space

overturned hurdle-back to start

false start back 1 space

jump move ahead 2 spaces

landed in pit-lose 1 turn

sand pit for broad jump

START

FINISH LINE WIN!

landed in pit-lose 1 turn

missed hurdle back 1 space

sand pit

good jump move ahead 1 space

BACK PACKER

MATERIALS

Poster board or oaktag, die, position markers, magic markers.

DIRECTIONS

Make a game board similar to the diagram, approximately 30" x 18". Number the spaces and write in sayings similar to those on the board. Other sayings might be:

    a. overnight camp—lose 1 turn
    b. fall in river—go back to 24
    c. by-passed fallen tree—go ahead to 38

Some spaces are not numbered. These are the short cut spaces.
Cut as many task cards as needed out of oaktag. Write words, sounds, math facts, etc., on the task cards. Make twenty short cut cards out of oaktag, approximately 2½" x 4". Write the following sayings on the short cut cards:

    five cards that read—free space (remain in same space)
    five cards that read—move ahead 2 spaces
    five cards that read—go back 2 spaces
    five cards that read—go back 1 space

SUGGESTED ACTIVITY

Place all position markers on start. The first player draws a task card. If he responds correctly, he rolls the die and moves the appropriate number of spaces on the board. If he responds incorrectly, he remains in the same position. When a child gets to a short cut path, he may choose to take the short cut or continue on the main path. If he chooses the short cut, the die is rolled as usual and the marker may be advanced the number of spaces that appears on the die. If the player lands on one of the unnumbered short cut spaces, a short cut card must be drawn. He must then follow the directions on the short cut card, thereby taking a risk.

BACK PACKER

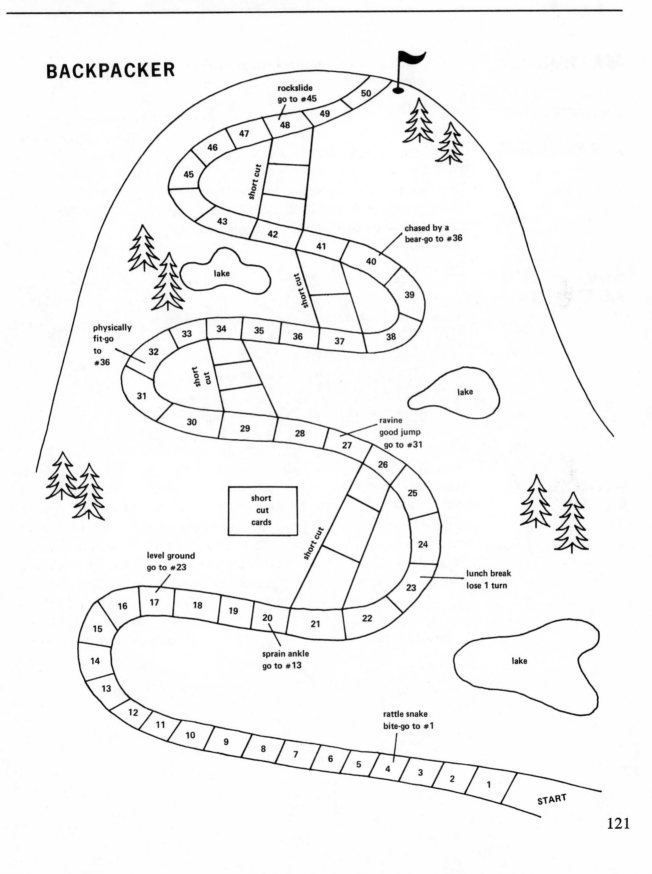

BACKPACKER

rockslide
go to #45

50

49

48

47

46

45

43

42

short cut

lake

41

40

chased by a
bear-go to #36

39

short cut

33 34 35 36 37 38

physically
fit-go
to
#36

32

short
cut

lake

31

30 29 28

27

ravine
good jump
go to #31

26

25

short
cut
cards

24

short cut

level ground
go to #23

23

lunch break
lose 1 turn

16 17 18 19 20 21 22

15

14

sprain ankle
go to #13

lake

13

12

11 10 9 8 7 6 5 4 3 2 1

rattle snake
bite-go to #1

START

121

SNEAKY SNAKEY

MATERIALS Poster board, magic markers, number 5 1¼″ brass round head fasteners, laminating equipment or clear contact paper, position markers, die numbered 1-6.

DIRECTIONS Cut the poster board into strips approximately 2′ long by 3″ wide. With the magic marker make spaces on the strips. Then laminate the strips and join them together with the fasteners to form a Sneaky Snakey path. The length of the game may be varied according to the number of strips that are fastened together.

SUGGESTED ACTIVITY Write words, sounds, math facts, etc., that are being studied in the spaces. If desired, some "Sneaky Snakey" sayings may be written on the path. For example:

> Snake bite—go back 1 space
> Rattler pit—jump ahead 1 space
> Slither—ahead 2 spaces
> Coil—back 1 space

Taking turns, each child rolls the die and moves his marker on the game board. He must respond correctly to the task in the space he lands on or go back to his previous position. The winner is the first child to reach the end of "Sneaky Snakey."

SNEAKY SNAKEY

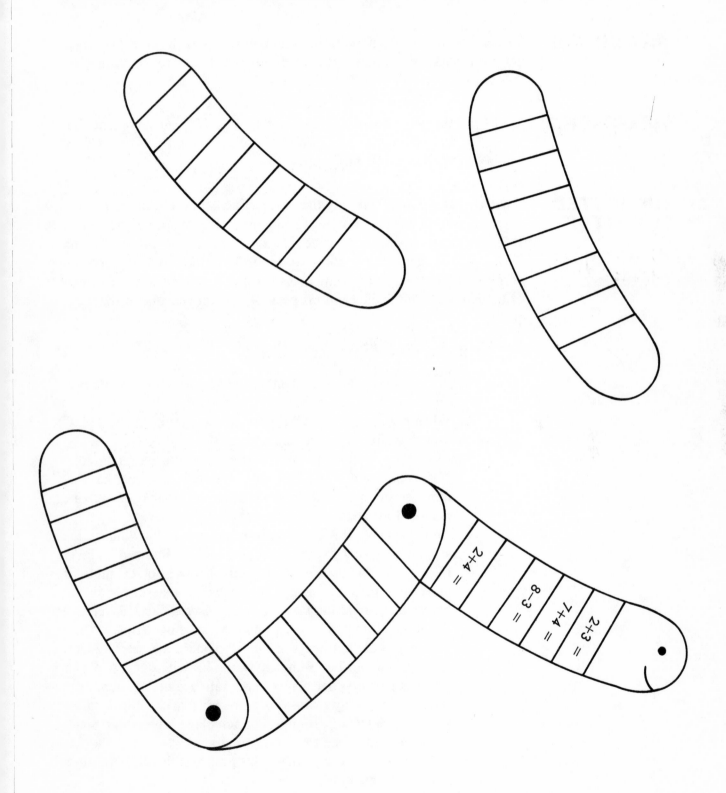

On the snake, the equations read:

2+4 =
8-3 =
7+4 =
2+3 =

BUMP OFF

MATERIALS Poster board, magic markers in four colors, thirty flash cards, eight position markers, two each of four different colors, two die numbered 1-6.

DIRECTIONS Construct the game board approximately 18″ x 18″, similar to the diagram. Write arithmetic facts, words, letters, etc., on the thirty flash cards or use commercial flash cards.

SUGGESTED ACTIVITY Two to four children can play the game. Each child begins by placing his two position markers on the starting arrows of the same color. For example, there would be two red markers on the red arrow. Taking turns, players must answer correctly the task on the top flash card, before rolling the dice and moving ahead. If the player answers incorrectly he may not roll the dice and his position marker remains in the same place.

The following rules guide the play on the Bump Off board:

a. Players must roll a six on either die to start a position marker on the Go space.

b. When both position markers are on the circular path, a player may choose to move one marker the total or both dice or move each marker the number indicated on one of the die. For example, if a player rolls a four and a three, he may move seven spaces with one marker or he may move one marker four spaces and one marker three spaces.

c. A player may "Bump Off" another player by landing on the same space that player occupies. The "Bumped" player must return his marker to his start arrow. For example, if player one rolls a four and player two is four spaces ahead, player one would land on the same space. Then player two would be "Bumped" back to his own starting arrow.

d. The half circle pathways around the board are safety zones. A player cannot be "Bumped" while in that zone. A player may not pass another player in the safety zone. At any given time a player may choose to move his marker into a safety zone to avoid being "Bumped." Each player's own Start space is also a safety zone for his own markers.

e. The winner is the first player to return both of his position markers to his finish space.

BUMP OFF

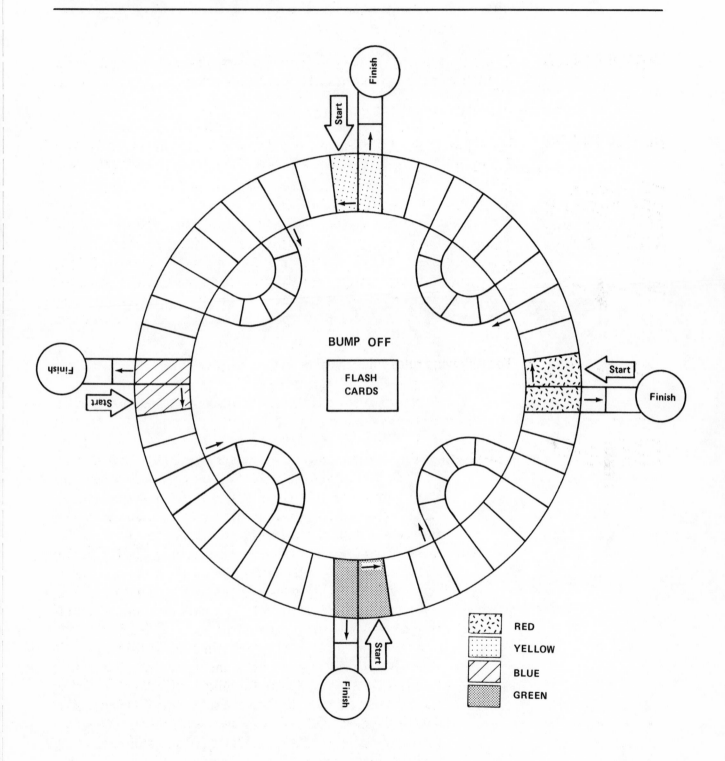

APPENDIX

DEFINITIONS

Appropriate for Secondary

Secondary refers to grades seven through twelve. Activities that are checked under the secondary column are so designated because their interest level is appropriate or can easily be adapted for the secondary grades.

Auditory Association

The organization process by which one is able to relate concepts presented auditorily.

Auditory Discrimination

The ability to hear the likenesses and differences among auditory stimuli—gross sounds; words; beginning, middle and ending sounds. The ability to distinguish between two different auditory stimuli.

Auditory Memory

The ability to retain input received auditorily.

Auditory Reception

The ability to derive meaning from material received auditorily.

Auditory Sequencing

Tasks in which one must reproduce auditorily received information in its proper sequence.

Fine-Motor

Activities or output in which precision in delicate muscle systems is required.

Gross-Motor

Activities or output in which groups of large muscles are used and the factor of strength may be important.

Learning Aptitudes

Refers to the basic abilities or responses required in a given instructional task. These abilities may involve both auditory and visual factors which are further broken down into specific component parts.

Manual Response

A non-verbal response such as writing, gestures, etc. in relation to a stimulus that is presented.

Sight Words

Sight words are words that do not follow the phonetic patterns and therefore cannot be decoded utilizing phonetic skills. A child recognizes sight words automatically when seen without analyzing the component parts.

Sound Blending

The ability to synthesize and combine the separate parts of a word and produce an integrated response.

Sound Symbol Relationships

The ability to associate or relate the sound unit with the visual symbol that represents it.

Verbal Response

A spoken/oral performance that is required in relation to a stimulus that is presented.

Visual Association

The organization process by which one is able to relate concepts presented visually.

Visual Closure

The ability to identify a visual stimulus from an incomplete visual presentation.

Visual Discrimination

The ability to see likenesses and differences among visual stimuli such as objects, pictures, forms, letters, words. It is seeing the essential elements of a visual stimulus. The ability to distinguish between two visual stimuli and to distinguish between the figure and the background of a visual field.

Visual Memory

The ability to retain input received visually.

Visual-Motor

Activities or output which require the ability to coordinate vision with movements of the body or parts of the body.

Visual Reception

The ability to gain meaning from information received visually.

Visual Sequencing

Tasks in which one must reproduce visually received information in its proper sequence.